InDesign® CS/CS2 KillerTips

MW01041184

INDESIGN® CS/CS2 KILLER TIPS

The InDesign® CS
Killer Tips Team

TECHNICAL EDITORS
Chris Main
Polly Reincheld

EDITOR
Richard Theriault

PRODUCTION EDITOR
Kim Gabriel

PRODUCTION
Dave Damstra
Dave Korman

COVER DESIGN AND
CREATIVE CONCEPTS
Felix Nelson

SITE DESIGN
Stacy Behan

Update for InDesign® CS2

EDITOR
Ted Waitt

PRODUCTION EDITOR
Connie Jeung-Mills

TECHNICAL REVIEW
Lynn Grillo

IMAGES
Kelly McCathran

COMPOSITOR
Owen Wolfson

PUBLISHED BY
New Riders

Copyright © 2006 by Scott Kelby

FIRST EDITION: September 2005

Composed in Myriad, Helvetica Black, and Cronos by NAPP Publishing

Trademarks
All terms mentioned in this book that are known to be trademarks or service marks have been appropriately capitalized. New Riders cannot attest to the accuracy of this information. Use of a term in the book should not be regarded as affecting the validity of any trademark or service mark.

InDesign is a registered trademark of Adobe Systems, Inc.
Windows is a registered trademark of Microsoft Corporation.

Warning and Disclaimer
This book is designed to provide information about InDesign tips. Every effort has been made to make this book as complete and as accurate as possible, but no warranty of fitness is implied.

The information is provided on an as-is basis. The authors and New Riders shall have neither liability nor responsibility to any person or entity with respect to any loss or damages arising from the information contained in this book or from the use of the discs or programs that may accompany it.

ISBN 0-321-33064-1

9 8 7 6 5 4 3 2 1

Printed and bound in the United States of America

www.peachpit.com
www.scottkelbybooks.com

*For my wonderful
wife Kalebra, for
enabling me to
marry the girl of
my dreams.*
—SCOTT KELBY

*For all designers
out there who
push the creative
envelope and
continue to design
great things.*
—TERRY WHITE

A NOTE ABOUT THIS BOOK

This book has been updated for InDesign CS2. With the exception of the final chapter, "What's New in InDesign CS2," the majority of the tips in this book are applicable in both CS and CS2.

ACKNOWLEDGMENTS

I learned a while back the real downside of being a co-author: You only get half as much space to thank all of the talented people who make a book like this possible.

First, I want to thank the most amazing woman I've ever known—my wife, Kalebra. You meet very few people in your life who are truly inspiring, truly giving, compassionate to a fault, and literally a joy to be around—and she is every one of those and more. She's my best friend, confidante, a world-class mom, gourmet chef, advice desk, and one heck of a savvy business woman. It's an absolute joy seeing her special gifts reflected in our son Jordan (who has no idea how blessed we both are to have her in our life).

I want to thank my co-author, Terry White, for agreeing to do this book with me. Besides being one of my very best friends, Terry knows more about InDesign than anyone I've ever known, so he was my first, and only, choice as this book's co-author. But Terry's much more than just an InDesign expert: He's a uniquely talented individual whose passion and dedication touch everything he does, and everyone he meets; and I'm truly honored to be able to work with him.

I want to thank my home team at KW Media Group, who constantly redefine what "kickin' butt" really means. In particular, I want to thank my Creative Director Felix Nelson; my Editor Richard Theriault; my Tech Editors Chris Main and Polly Reincheld; and Production Editor Kim Gabriel. Also thanks to Barbara Thompson, Dave Korman, Daphne Durkee, and Dave "The Michigan Layout Machine" Damstra. I'd put them up against any production team in the business—they're that good.

I also want to thank wonderful, crazy, loving Dad Jerry for being so "him," and thanks to my brother Jeff for having so much "him" in him. Thanks to my friends and business partners, Jim Workman and Jean A. Kendra, and thanks to coach Joe Gibbs for coming back to the Redskins, which is better than anything I could say or do for my absolutely wonderful Executive Assistant Kathy Siler.

Thanks to Nancy Ruenzel, Scott Cowlin, Kim Lombardi, Gary Paul Prince, and everyone at Peachpit for their commitment to excellence, and for the honor of letting me be one of their "Voices That Matter."

And most importantly, an extra special thanks to God and his son Jesus Christ for always hearing my prayers, for always being there when I need Him, and for blessing me with a life I truly love, and a warm loving family to share it with.

—*SCOTT KELBY*

....

Co-authoring this book would not have been possible if not for the continued inspiration and support of my friends, family, and colleagues. While there aren't enough pages to thank and acknowledge everyone, I would like to acknowledge my wife Carla, who has constantly supported my efforts; my two daughters Ayoola and Sala, both visions of beauty and motivation; my sister Pam, who is always there for me to bounce ideas and problems off of; and of course, my mom and dad.

I would like to thank all my friends, team members, managers, and colleagues at Adobe, including Sue Scheen, Lynn Grillo, Adam Pratt, Mike Richman, Colin Smith, Steve Whatley, Noha Edell, Ashwini Jambotkar, Gary Cosimini, Lisa Forrester, Tim Cole, Julieanne Kost, Rye Livingston, Diane Olson, Peggy Snyder, Russell Preston Brown, Dave Helmly, Jim Ringham, Rick Borstein, Donna Zontos, Lisa Avalos, the entire Americas Sales Team, and the InDesign Product Team.

I would also like to thank all my friends in the Mac community for their continued support and help over the years, especially Steve Wozniak, Sandy Kaye, Calvin Carson, Mia Sasser, Mike Arlow, Mary and Joseph Grey, Carmela Z. Robertson, Shirley Kussner, Chita Hunter, Lori Autrey, Lesa Snider, Phyllis Evans, David Syme, Leonard Mazerov, Kwesi Ohene Aquil, and Piankhi Blount.

Last but certainly not least, I would like to especially thank Scott Kelby and the folks at KW Media Group for the opportunity to collaborate on this project. I would also like to thank all InDesign users worldwide.

—*TERRY WHITE*

ABOUT THE AUTHORS

Scott Kelby

Scott is Editor-in-Chief and co-founder of *Photoshop User* magazine, Editor-in-Chief of Nikon's *Capture User* magazine, and Editor-in-Chief of *Layers* magazine. He is President of the National Association of Photoshop Professionals (NAPP), the trade association for Adobe® Photoshop® users, and he's President of KW Media Group, Inc., a Florida-based software education and publishing firm.

Scott is author of the best-selling books *Photoshop CS Down & Dirty Tricks, The Photoshop CS2 Book for Digital Photographers,* and *Photoshop CS2 Killer Tips* and he's creator and Series Editor for the Killer Tips series of books from New Riders.

Scott is Training Director for the Adobe Photoshop Seminar Tour, Conference Technical Chair for the PhotoshopWorld Conference & Expo, and he is a speaker at graphics trade shows and events around the world. He is also featured in a series of Adobe Photoshop training DVDs and has been training creative professionals since 1993.

For more background info on Scott, visit www.scottkelby.com.

Terry White

Terry White, Technical Resources Manager–Adobe Systems Inc., is a technologist at heart. He loves computers and all things tech. Terry has been with Adobe for seven years, and has extensive knowledge of Adobe's Creative Professional product line. In his current position as Technical Resources Manager for North America, he leads a team of Applications Engineers who focus on professional publishing, Web authoring, and digital video. Terry has been active in the industry for over 18 years and is the founder and president of MacGroup-Detroit—Michigan's largest Macintosh Users group—and a columnist for *Layers* magazine.

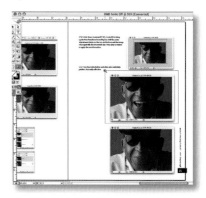

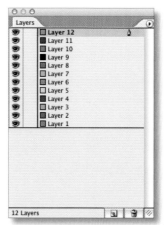

TABLE OF CONTENTS

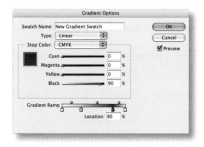

TABLE OF CONTENTS

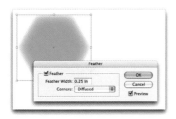

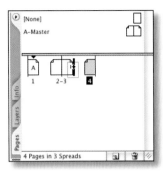

TABLE OF CONTENTS

TABLE OF CONTENTS

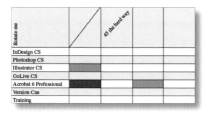

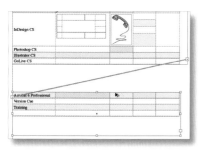

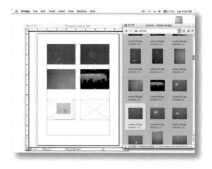

TABLE OF CONTENTS

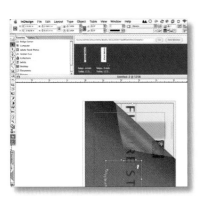

IF YOU'RE THINKING THIS IS THE INTRODUCTION, YOU'RE WAY OFF BASE

TIP

*This is a sidebar tip. Every great computer book has a few of them. But this book is nothing **but** them. A whole book of cool sidebar tips, without the sidebars.*

That's because this book has no introduction.
We're not saying "it needs no introduction." This book desperately needs an introduction. It's crying out for an introduction—begging for one (if you will), but we sat down and intentionally decided not to write one. Why? Because we have mental problems. Deep-rooted psychological problems that will probably one day become the syllabus for college-level study. Why? Why would two men of otherwise unremarkable lives decide to go against time-honored traditions, which all book publishers hold sacred, and not write an introduction? Well, we'll tell you—it's because nobody reads introductions. Nobody. Not you. Not us. Nobody. See, you're not reading one now.

So why do authors even write introductions?
Their publishers force them to. It's true. They're forced to write an introduction, even though the publishing company knows full well that no one will read it, not even editors from the publishing company itself. Here's an example: "We were going to right an entroduction; but know one kares enuff to chech it." See—an editor would never let that slip by, but they don't even run introductions by part-time interns. Yet there it is—in print—in a book from a major computer book publishing company (at least they were until this book hit the shelves). Are we concerned? Nah. They'll never learn that a severely messed-up sentence wound up in the published version of the book, because that would require having a least one person read it; and you know darn well that person doesn't exist.

Why do books need an introduction, anyway?
We have no idea. Okay, it's probably so the authors can tell the reader how to use the book (we assume it's stuff like "Once you reach the bottom of a right-facing page, turn the page to continue," but since we don't read introductions, that's purely a guess). On the other hand, if we *were* to write an introduction (and don't worry, we're not) we'd probably tell you what makes this book different from other books.

What makes this book different from other books?
Well, it has a road sign on the cover, and most books don't. Besides that, the one thing that makes this book different is that the whole book, cover-to-cover, is just tips. Tips to make you more efficient, faster, and have more fun while you're using InDesign. There are no detailed descriptions of how to check out managed documents over a workgroup server, or how to adjust the Hyphenation Zone (we know you're disappointed, because those two sound like a lot of fun)—instead, we cut through the bull and give you nothing but the inside shortcuts, cool workarounds, and proven tricks that help you get twice the work done in half the time. The stuff that makes you faster, better, and worth more to your clients and your company.

Do we really need to work faster?
Yes. Next question.

Come on. Is working faster that important?

It's *that* important. Nobody wants to do things "the hard way." The slow way. The frustrating way. Your time is important, and if you're working more efficiently in InDesign, you'll have time for other important things like trying different layouts, exploring creative possibilities, and maybe even a dinner break. That's what this book is all about. Other books sprinkle a few sidebar tips throughout their pages, but this book is nothing but those sidebar tips.

What's a sidebar?

It's one of those gray boxes on the left and right of this spread, with the word "TIP" at the top. That's how most books handle tips—in a box, in the sidebar of the book. As cool as those sidebar tips are, there are two problems: (1) There are never enough of them, and (2) those tips are usually in just a tiny little box with a couple of lines of text (like the sidebar shown at right). So in this book, we include literally hundreds of tips, and we thought we'd expand the explanations enough to make them more accessible, and then add a screen capture if (a) it helps make the tip easier to understand, or (b) if the page just looks really boring without one.

So what exactly is a "Killer Tip"?

"Use the Type tool to create type." Technically, that is a tip. It's a lame tip. It's a boringly obvious tip, and it's definitely not a Killer Tip. To be a "Killer Tip" it's supposed to make you nod and smile when you read it. A Killer Tip is one that you can't wait to show off to your page-layout buddies, because you'll look like the big pro and they'll look like the big schmo. (Schmo is one of those words that doesn't make it into enough computer books. Why? Because editors remove words like "schmo" from all non-introduction areas. It's what they do for fun.)

Is this book for you?

If you've come this far, knowing all the while that you were indeed reading what some might call "The book's introduction" (not Terry and I mind you, some other people—bad people), then this book is absolutely for you. However, if you had no idea—you were completely unaware, either consciously or subconsciously, that you were in fact reading the book's introduction—then we're afraid you may be somewhat gullible and therefore in danger of being taken advantage of and we want to protect you from that by having you buy this book, and paying the bookstore twice the published price (hey, it's worth a shot).

Okay, how do I get started?

This book isn't set up like a novel—you can jump in anywhere, start on any page and immediately try the tips that interest you most. Also, don't forget to read each chapter's intro page—it's critical to your understanding of what's in that particular chapter (that's totally not true, but it took a long time to write those intros, so we use little lies like this to get you to read them. Sad, isn't it?).

Wait! One last thing!

Actually, there's nothing else. Gotcha! Okay, now turn the page and get to "tippin'!"

TIP

You're doing it again! Stop looking at these sidebars. See, they're intoxicating—you're drawn to them even after you know it's not really a tip. Okay, here's a real tip: If you like sidebar tips, buy this book.

Who's Zoomin' Who

NAVIGATING AND
OTHER ESSENTIALS

Since we (and by "we" I mean "me") spend so much of our lives (which is to say "mine") navigating through documents, it would save us loads of time each day if we

Who's Zoomin' Who
navigating and other essentials

were to get incredibly efficient at navigating. Now, what would we do with all that extra time? Would we go home early? Spend more time with our family? Nope. We'd do what designers love doing best—zooming. When no one's around, we zoom in and out of our documents repeatedly. We zoom in to a 400% view, then back out to 50%; in to a 1200% view, and back out to 12.5%. Why? Nobody knows. Scientists have studied this for years, and still—nothin'. I think it's a power thing. Maybe that's why there are about a gazillion ways to zoom, magnify, nudge, and otherwise move through our InDesign pages. We (and by "we" I mean "you") secretly love the power of knowing that at any given time, for no apparent reason, we can zoom in to a 4000% enlargement of one character of text. It's weird. It's annoying. But we love it (by "we" I mean "you," and by "it" I mean "it").

UNDO A ZOOM? YOU CAN WITH THIS HIDDEN SHORTCUT

Here's one of those hidden shortcuts that are incredibly handy, but we've met so few people who know them that hardly anyone uses them (of course, you'll start using this one now, and that's a good thing). Once you've zoomed in on something, you know there's no "undo" for zooming. Or is there? You can toggle between your current view and your zoomed-in view by pressing Option-Command-2 (PC: Alt-Control-2). This is another one of those tips that you'll try once, and then use it again and again.

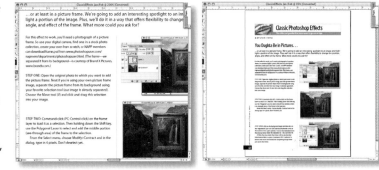

   SET YOUR OWN DEFAULTS

Want your default font to be different? Want the default stroke to be .5 instead of 1 point? Want the default Text Wrap to be Wrap Around Bounding Box? It's easy to set the overall defaults—you just have to know this one thing—set them all while there is no document open. That's right, close all your open documents, make all your changes, then these new changes become your defaults. Freaky, I know.

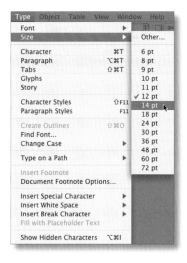

THE "JUMP TO ANY PAGE" SHORTCUT

If you're working on a multipage document and you know which page you want to jump to, we've got a very fast way to get there. Just press Command-J (PC: Control-J) and the Page Number field highlights. Enter the page number, then press Enter and BAM—you're there. If you're trying to get to a master page (and you know the name of the master page you want), use the same shortcut but instead of entering a number, just type in the first few letters of the master page and it will jump to that page.

   ## GET TO THE FIRST PAGE FAST!

Want to jump directly to the first page in your document? We're not talking about the page you have auto-numbered as page 1, because if you're working on a book or a magazine, that could well be page 354. Nope, we're talking about jumping to the actual first page in your document. To jump right there, press Command-J (PC: Control-J) to highlight the Page Number field, then type "+1" and press Enter to jump to the very first page.

OPEN OR CLOSE ALL YOUR SIDE TAB PALETTES WITH ONE CLICK

Want to open (or close) all of the side tab palettes at once, with just one click? Just hold the Option key (PC: Alt key), then click on any open side palette's tab and they'll all open (or close) at once. Pretty darn handy.

   SPEED TIP: HIGHLIGHTING FIELDS

Want to highlight a field fast? Just click once on the icon for that field and it will automatically highlight the value that's currently there. This saves a bunch of time because once you click, you can immediately type in a new value to replace the old one. Plus, not only is this a faster way to select a field, it's easier than trying to get your cursor in those tiny fields, and then highlight the numbers. Try this once—you'll use it again and again.

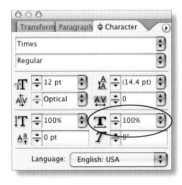

NEW DOCS WITHOUT THE NEW DOCUMENT DIALOG

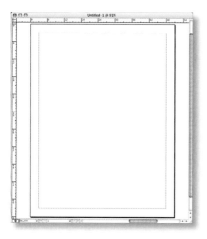

Want another new document that's the same size and specs as the last document you created? Just press Option-Command-N (PC: Alt-Control-N) and the new doc will instantly appear, based on the settings you last used—no New Document dialog, no muss, no fuss.

   ## RESET THE NEW DOCUMENT DIALOG

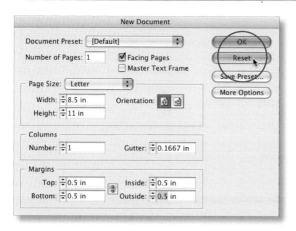

If you're entering values in the New Document dialog, and you change your mind or make a mistake, you don't have to hit the Cancel button and start all over. Instead, just hold the Option key (PC: Alt key) and you'll see the Cancel button change into the Reset button. Click it, and it will return all the settings to what they were when you opened it.

SAVE TIME WHEN CREATING NEW DOCUMENTS

If you find yourself creating new documents in a non-standard size (for example, rather than letter-size documents, perhaps you create 6x4″ postcards fairly often), you can create and save your own custom preset size and have it appear in the Document Preset pop-up menu in the New Document dialog. Here's how: Go under the File menu, under New, and choose Document. In the New Document dialog, enter your own custom width, height, margins, etc., and then click the Save Preset button (as shown) and a dialog will

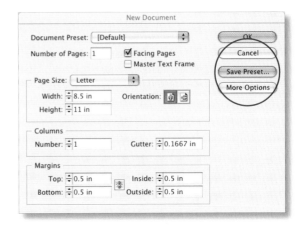

appear where you can name your new document preset. When you click OK, this new preset will appear in the Document Preset pop-up menu.

   ## SEE YOUR WHOLE SPREAD ONSCREEN

If you're working on a spread and press the shortcut for Fit Page in Window (Command-Zero [PC: Control-Zero]) it will fit the entire height of your page in the window, but you'll probably have to scroll to the right or left to see your entire spread. That is, unless you press Option-Command-Zero (PC: Alt-Control-Zero) instead, which gives you Fit Spread in Window rather than just Fit Page in Window.

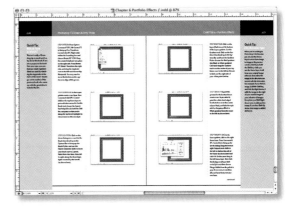

FIT SPREAD IN WINDOW EVEN FASTER!

If you want an even faster way to see your full page or spread as large as possible on your monitor (see previous tip), save yourself a trip all the way up to the View menu in the menu bar or using the Command-Option-Zero (PC: Control-Alt-Zero) shortcut, and instead just double-click directly on the Hand tool in the Toolbox and it'll jump right to the Fit Spread in Window view.

   NOT JUST THE PAGE OR SPREAD—SEE THE WHOLE PASTEBOARD

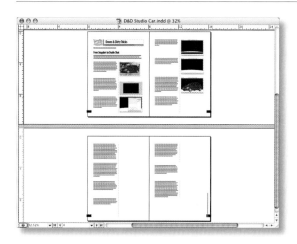

If you're anything like us (and we feel you are), you use the pasteboard area outside your page to store things you think you might need later (like extra blocks of text, photos, logos, etc.). But if you're like us, then you probably lose track of which page you were on when you placed those things just beyond your page borders. If that's the case, just press Shift-Option-Command-Zero (PC: Shift-Alt-Control-Zero) to see the entire pasteboard fitted to your screen.

SPEED ZOOMING

Our favorite way to zoom in to and out of our document doesn't use the Zoom tool at all. Instead, we feel the fastest way is to press Command–+ (PC: Control–+) to quickly zoom in, and then Command-minus sign (PC: Control-minus sign) to zoom out. With each press, your view zooms in (or out, depending on which shortcut you use), and it's so fast, it'll probably wind up being your favorite way too!

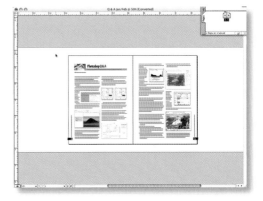

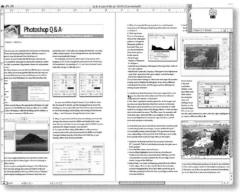

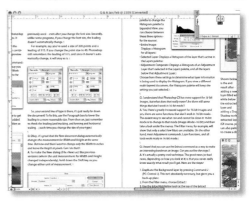

THE SPEEDWAY TO A 100% VIEW

Want to see your document at its full 100% size? Just double-click directly on the Zoom tool (magnifying glass) in the Toolbox. Don't get the tool, just double-click on it.

JUMP TO A 200% ENLARGEMENT OF WHERE YOU'RE WORKING

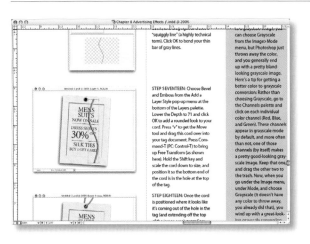

If you want to jump quickly to a 200% view of the area right where you're working in your document, you're just one keystroke away. As long as you've clicked on anything in that area (an object, some type, anything), you can press Command-2 (PC: Control-2) and you'll be zoomed into that exact area at a 200% magnification.

THE SECRET ZOOM FIELD SHORTCUT

If you know exactly the percentage amount
you want to zoom in (or out), you can
highlight the Zoom field (in the bottom left
corner of your document window) and type
in the amount. However, if it seems like a
lot of trouble to head down there, highlight

the field manually, and then type in the percentage, you'll love this tip: Just press Option-
Command-5 (PC: Alt-Control-5) and the field will highlight automatically. All you do is type
in your desired percentage, then press Enter. You don't even have to type the percentage
symbol, just type in the number, hit the Enter key, and it zooms!

   BETTER NAVIGATION WHILE ZOOMED IN

If you've zoomed in close on
your document, there's a much
easier way to navigate around
your document than trying
to use the scroll bars. Instead,
once you're zoomed in, just
hold Option-Spacebar (PC:
Alt-Spacebar) and your current
tool temporarily changes to
the Hand tool, so you can click
within your document area
and move the document right
where you want it. When you're
done navigating, just release
the keys and you're right back
to the tool you were last using.

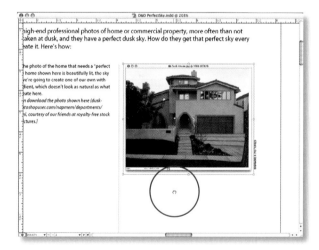

SWITCH TO THE ZOOM TOOL TEMPORARILY

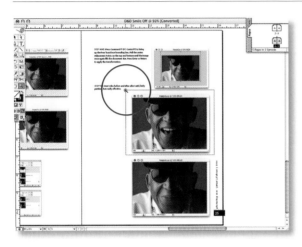

Anytime you want to zoom in on a precise area, you can temporarily switch from the tool you're using to the Zoom tool by holding Command-Spacebar (PC: Control-Spacebar). When you release the keys, you're back to the tool you were originally using. To zoom out, add the Option key (PC: Alt key) to the shortcut.

CHOOSE WHEN YOUR BASELINE GRID IS VISIBLE

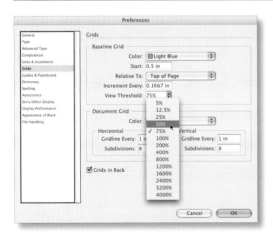

If you use the Baseline Grid feature (under the View menu, choose Show Baseline Grid), you can decide at which page magnifications this grid remains visible. For example, by default if you zoom out to less than a 75% view, the once-visible grid is hidden. However, if you want to still see the grid at smaller magnifications, you can control the "threshold" at which it's visible by going under InDesign (PC: Edit), under Preferences, under Grids, and lowering the View Threshold amount. I have to say—that's pretty slick.

   THOSE PESKY RULER GUIDES

Ruler guides can be a blessing and they can be a pain. That's why there's an option to hide them. However, manually hiding ruler guides and then showing them can be frustrating too. In

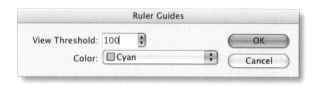

most cases you want to see the guides when you're zoomed in and not when you're zoomed out. You can control that "threshold" just like you can for the Baseline Grid (see previous tip). Before you drag out your guides, choose Ruler Guides from the Layout menu and change the View Threshold to 100%. Now when you drag new guides onto the page, they will be visible only when you're zoomed in to 100% or greater. When you're zoomed out to 99% or less they will disappear.

   YOUR TOOLBOX, YOUR WAY

Don't like the default tall, two-column Toolbox? No sweat. Just double-click the little tab at the very top of the Toolbox (circled in red here), and the bar will switch to a single-row vertical Toolbox (shown at far right). Double-click it again, and it will switch to a horizontal single-row bar (shown below). How do you get back to the default, two-column vertical Toolbox? Just double-click that little tab one more time.

Single-row horizontal

Double-row vertical

Single-row vertical

FLOAT THE CONTROL PALETTE

Although the Control palette is docked at the top of your screen by default, it doesn't have to be that way. You can make it a floating palette by clicking directly on the little vertical tab on the far left of it and just dragging it off. If you want to dock it at the bottom of your screen, click on that little tab again (not the end of the palette, the little tab just to the right of it, shown here circled in red) and drag it to the bottom left-hand corner of your screen.

 SHRINK THE CONTROL PALETTE

If you decide that you like floating the Control palette, rather than having it docked at the top of the screen, so it stays out of the way (see previous tip), you're really going to love this tip: Once it's floating, if you double-click on the far left tab, the entire bar will tuck away, leaving only a small floating tab. To see the Control palette again, double-click on the tab again.

MANAGE PALETTE CLUTTER

Although the side tab palette concept of InDesign goes a long way to help keep your screen free of palettes, there are some other things you can do to minimize your palette clutter. First, if you see small, double-headed black arrows in the palette's tab, right before the palette's name, you can click on those arrows to expand or collapse the palette's extra options (as shown in the middle capture here). If you really want to save some space, double-click directly on a palette's tab and it "tucks up" so that just the tab remains visible. Even if you have nested palettes (more than one palette grouped together), double-clicking on any of their tabs tucks them all up. To reveal the full palette(s), just double-click on the tab again.

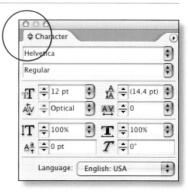

Full-sized palette

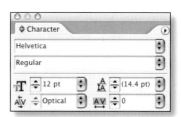

Options hidden

Just the tabs

FIT MORE IN YOUR LAYERS PALETTE

If you're working with a lot of layers, your Layers palette can get pretty full pretty quick. But there's a trick you can use to help see more layers without making the Layers palette larger (and believe me, making the palette take up more space is not our goal). To fit more layers in your Layers palette, choose Small Palette Rows from the palette's flyout menu. In the example shown here, the regular palette (shown left) lets you access all of your layers; but by choosing Small Palette Rows, you are able to add—and see—many more layers at once.

   MAKE AN ÜBER-PALETTE

Adobe has devised a number of different ways to reduce palette clutter, but some people (you know who you are) want the opposite—all their favorite palettes visible all the time in one big palette (we call this an "über-palette"). Here's how to make your own: Once you've nested three or four of your favorite palettes together, open another palette, grab its name, and drag it to the bottom of your main palette. Move it around until a black highlight bar appears along the bottom of the top palette (you have to line up the tip of your mouse with the bottom of the palette). Release your mouse button, and this palette will "dock" vertically to the bottom of your top palette, which is the beginning of your own über-palette. Keep docking more palettes to the bottom or nesting more palettes until all your favorites are visible in one long palette (like the one shown here).

SET YOUR WORKSPACE ONCE, AND IT'S YOURS FOREVER!

When you first launch InDesign, all the palettes, Toolbox, etc. are in their default positions (basically, they're where Adobe decided they'd be), but you can just as easily set up your own custom workspace so that every time you work, all the palettes, Toolbox, etc. are right where you want them, with only the

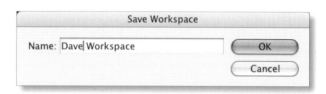

palettes you want visible. To do this, first, put everything where you want it (in other words, set up your workspace your way). Then go under the Window menu, under Workspace, and choose Save Workspace. A dialog will appear where you can name your workspace. Click OK, then to get to your custom workspace anytime, just go under the Window menu, under Workspace, and choose your named workspace. Saving your own custom workspace is ideal for anyone who shares a computer with other users, or for anyone who likes different setups for different tasks.

   HIDE ALL PALETTES AND TOOLBOX WITH ONE CLICK

When the palette clutter really gets to you (and believe me, it will), and you want a clean, completely uncluttered view of your document, just press the Tab key on your keyboard; and every palette, even your Toolbox, will be hidden from view. Once the blood returns to your head, you can press Tab again to bring them all back.

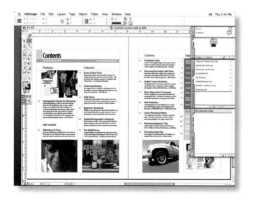 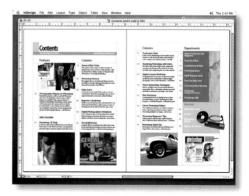

ONE CLICK HIDES PALETTES, BUT LEAVES TOOLBOX VISIBLE

Want to hide all your palettes, but keep the Toolbox visible? With no items selected in your document, click the little palette icon in the Control palette (circled here in red) and you're there! If you do have any items selected, this will cycle the appropriate palettes for that object.

HIDE JUST PALETTES

Even though the side tabs of InDesign only take up a tiny bit of space, sometimes even that is too much and you just want them out of the way. If you want to hide your palettes, but leave your Control palette and Toolbox still visible, just press Shift-Tab and they'll hide until you press Shift-Tab again. When will you use this little shortcut most? Probably to reach the vertical scroll bar on the right side of your document window (at least, that's when we use it).

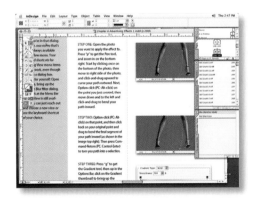 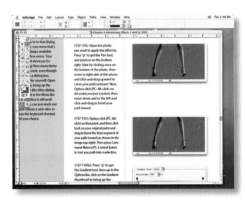

SIDE-TAB A GROUP OF PALETTES

What happens if you have three palettes nested together, and you drag one of those tabs over to the right side of your screen to make it a side tab? Well, sadly only that particular palette becomes a side tab—the others that were nested with it just remain onscreen. Don't you wish there was a way you could nest all three palettes at once, instead of one at a time? There is: Hold Option (PC: Alt) before you drag the tab, then all the palettes will become side tabs as a group.

   HOW TO PREVIEW YOUR DOCUMENT

If at any time you want a preview of how your document will look, without all the guides, non-printing elements, etc., you can click on the Preview Mode button at the bottom of the Toolbox (or press the letter "w" on your keyboard when you're not in the Type tool), and you'll get the clean unfettered view. If you've added slugs or bleeds, there are special previews that will show them as well, just choose those views from the Preview Mode flyout menu (as shown here).

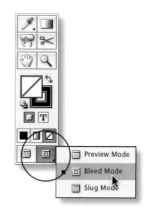

SAVE EVERY OPEN DOCUMENT WITH ONE KEYSTROKE

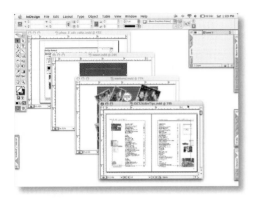

If you have a number of different documents open and you have a sneaking suspicion that your system's getting ready to take a dive (i.e., crash), here's a keyboard shortcut that can save your life (okay, it's a lifesaver, but it won't actually save your life). Just press Shift-Option-Command-S (PC: Shift-Alt-Control-S) and every open document will be saved. Nothing like a one-keystroke insurance policy, eh?

   ## A BIGGER VIEW IN THE NAVIGATOR PALETTE

This one surprises a lot of people who always use the tiny Navigator palette at its default size (left picture). If you want a larger preview in the Navigator palette, it resizes like a window—just grab the bottom right-hand corner and drag it out. As the palette's window gets bigger, so does the thumbnail of your page (right picture).

 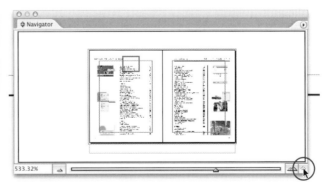

I WANT TO SEE IT ALL

The Navigator palette is sweet for being able to see your entire spread at one time and to zoom in on specific areas; but with today's monitors you can pretty much accomplish that anyway. Don't give up on the Navigator, though. Choose View All Spreads from the Navigator palette's flyout menu. Now you can see all the spreads in one view and navigate to any spot in your document with a click-and-drag.

THE FIVE MOST IMPORTANT ONE-KEY TOOL SHORTCUTS

Want to start saving loads of time every single day? Then learn these five easy-to-remember one-key shortcuts, so you can switch to the most popular tools quickly.

Selection Tool: V   *Line Tool: *   *Type Tool: T*   *Pen Tool: P*   *Direct Selection Tool: A*
                         (backslash)

Learn just those five, and you'll be amazed at how much your efficiency improves.

NO KEYBOARD SHORTCUT? MAKE ONE!

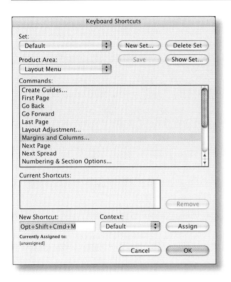

If you find yourself using a command that doesn't have a keyboard shortcut (like the Margins and Columns dialog, for example), then just make one. Go under the Edit menu and choose Keyboard Shortcuts. When the dialog appears, from the Product Area pop-up choose whichever menu the command appears under (in the example shown here, Margins and Columns appears under the Layout Menu). Then in the list of commands that appears, click on the command that you want to assign a keyboard shortcut (as shown here). If there's already a shortcut, it will appear in the Current Shortcuts window. If not, add your own: Click once in the New Shortcut field, then type in the keystrokes of the shortcut you want to use, click Assign, then click OK. Cool!

 COMING OVER FROM QUARKXPRESS? USE QUARK SHORTCUTS

If you're coming to InDesign after leaving QuarkXPress (in fact, I'd guess most people using InDesign did just that), you can make the transition easier by having InDesign load all of QuarkXPress's same keyboard shortcuts. That way, you don't have to relearn how to do, well…everything. Here's how to load 'em: Go under the Edit menu and choose Keyboard Shortcuts. When the dialog appears, choose Shortcuts for QuarkXPress 4.0 from the Set pop-up menu at the top of the dialog (as shown here) and then click OK. That's all there is to it. (Note: Changing this makes an excellent prank to pull on co-workers. Not that you'd ever do it, but wouldn't it be hilarious to watch them as they learn that none of their keyboard shortcuts seem to work? Hmmmmm.)

PRINT YOUR CUSTOM KEYBOARD SHORTCUTS

If you've decided to add your own custom set of keyboard shortcuts to InDesign, how are you going to remember them all? You don't have to—just print out your custom set by going under the Edit menu and choosing Keyboard Shortcuts. Then in the dialog, click on the Show Set button (as shown) and it will launch your text editor and display a list of all the keyboard shortcuts in your set (as shown here), which you can then print as a reference. How sweet is that?

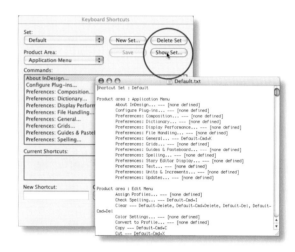

   BRING BACK THOSE HIDDEN WARNING DIALOGS

Chances are you've had a warning dialog pop up more than once. And if you have, chances are you've clicked on the checkbox that says something along the lines of "Don't show again." However, sure enough, at some point you'll want to remember what that warning said (or perhaps now you're sharing your computer with someone else, and you want him to see the warning). To get those scary warning dialogs back, go under the InDesign menu (PC: Edit menu), under Preferences, to General, and at the bottom of the dialog click the Reset All Warning Dialogs button (as shown). Then click OK.

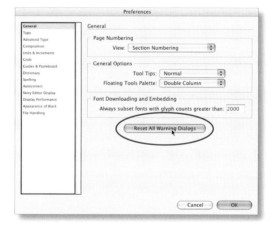

Stereo
Type

TWEAKIN' YOUR TEXT

If there's one area where InDesign undeniably reigns supreme, it's type tweaking. You can flat-out set some seriously righteous type in this program; and

Stereo Type
tweakin' your text

it's packed with so many high-end typographic features that I'm not sure that even Adobe knows what half of them do. But here's the thing: If you take the time to learn some of these type tips, not only will you work faster and smarter, but you'll also be well on your way to becoming a total type snob. Once you reach that lofty plane, ah my friend, life will be sweet. You'll look down on people who set type for coupons, newspaper ads, flyers, and other such nonsense. You'll laugh at their lack of ligatures. You'll scoff at their un-hung punctuation. You'll cackle at their non-curly quotes while you hiss and glare at them with the utter disdain, contempt, and loathing they deserve. They're beneath you. They're "double-spacers" and they should be dealt with accordingly. But even though you openly mock them, somewhere deep inside your soul, in a place you seldom dare venture, you know that before this chapter you, too, were one of them. An "under-liner." A "no-superscripter." A (dare I say it?) "non-kerner."

THE TYPE TOOL SUPER SHORTCUT

If you've got a layout with text frames in place on your page, when you decide to enter some text in a particular frame you don't have to go to the Toolbox to switch to the Type tool. Instead, when you have either of the Selection tools, just double-click inside any visible text frame. You'll immediately switch to the Type tool, and your cursor will be in place, ready for you to type.

  THE HIDDEN OPTIONS FOR TYPE ON A PATH

Want more control over how your type on a path works? Then go to the Toolbox and just double-click directly on the Type on a Path tool to bring up its options. (Note: To get to the Type on a Path tool, click-and-hold on the Type tool in the Toolbox, then

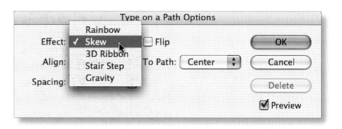

choose the Type on a Path tool from the flyout menu.) Perhaps one of the coolest options is the Effect pop-up menu, where you can apply different type-on-a-path effects, even after the type is already on the path.

SET YOUR TYPE DEFAULTS

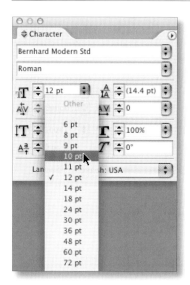

You can set the type defaults (default font, size, etc.) for your document very easily. Just make sure nothing is selected (to make sure, go under the Edit menu and choose Deselect All). Then get the Type tool, go to the Character palette and set everything the way you want it, and those now become your defaults. See, we told you it was easy.

   SET DEFAULT CHARACTER AND PARAGRAPH STYLES

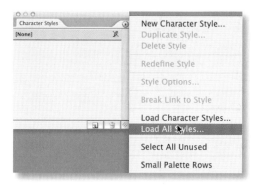

You can set default styles, and the easiest way is to import styles from an existing document that already has the styles you want. Here's how: First make sure no documents are open. Then go under the Type menu and choose Character Styles or Paragraph Styles—doesn't matter which. Then from the palette's flyout menu choose Load All Styles. This brings up a standard Open A File dialog. Navigate your way to your existing document that has the styles you want to use as your defaults,

then click Open. That's it—the styles from that document are now imported, and those styles are now your default paragraph and character styles.

   FAST FONT SIZE CHANGES FROM THE KEYBOARD

When it comes to resizing your fonts, save yourself trips to the Control palette or the Character palette and use these shortcuts instead. To jump up 2 point sizes at a time, highlight your text and press Shift-Command-> (PC: Shift-Control->). Perfect for making quick little adjustments. To make your highlighted type shrink by 2 points at a pop, press Shift-Command-< (PC: Shift-Control-<).

   JUMPING UP 2 POINTS AT A TIME NOT ENOUGH FOR YOU?

When using the shortcut in the previous tip, you may find that jumping up only 2 points at a time (the default) just isn't enough for you. You may want to jump to 6 points, 8, or even 10 points every time you press that shortcut. If that's the case, go under the InDesign menu (PC: Edit menu), under Preferences, and choose Units & Increments. In the Keyboard Increments section, under the Size/Leading field you'll see 2 entered as the current amount. You know what to do from here, right? Right!

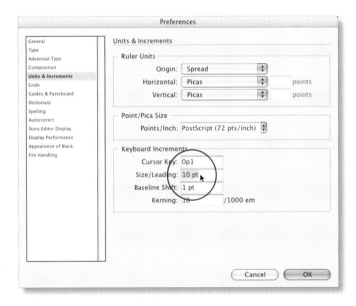

WAITING ON THE REAL TEXT? FAKE IT

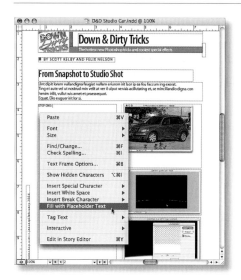

Many times when you're creating a layout for a publication, book, or print ad, you don't have the final copy (or any copy, for that matter) to use in your layout. But that doesn't have to stop you, because you can have InDesign add "dummy" text to flow into your text columns. Here's how: Create your columns, then Control-click (PC: Right-click) in your text frame and choose Fill With Placeholder Text from the pop-up menu that appears. The frame will be filled with sample text that you can use for layout purposes until the final text is delivered from the writers (and writers are always late—just ask any editor).

   ## TIP FOR MAGAZINE AND NEWSPAPER EDITORS

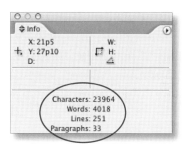

If you're working on a magazine or newspaper, you're working with writers; and chances are you're in charge of giving them (or at the very least, your editors) the word counts for their articles. If that's the case, InDesign can help. Put your text frames in place on the page where the article will appear, then go under the Type menu and choose Fill With Placeholder Text to fill the text frames with sample text. Now all you have to do is look at InDesign's built-in word count, which is found by going under the Window menu and choosing Info. At the bottom of the Info palette, you'll find the "counts," and the second one down is the word count for your selected text. (Note: If you don't see this information, it's just hidden. Go to the Info palette's flyout menu and choose Show Options.)

MAKE YOUR OWN CUSTOM PLACEHOLDER TEXT

If you don't like what InDesign's built-in placeholder text says, you can create your own custom placeholder text and use it instead. Just open the text file you want to use in your word processing application, then save that file and name it Placeholder.txt. Lastly, just drop that file in the InDesign folder. That's it—now it will use your custom text as the placeholder text.

Placeholder.txt

   CONTROL PALETTE STUNTS
(SWAPPING TYPE AND PARAGRAPH FIELDS)

When you have the Type tool, you can pull a pretty handy Control palette stunt that lets you decide whether the Control palette displays type attributes or paragraph attributes. Just press Option-Command-7 (PC: Alt-Control-7) and it swaps between the two Control palette layouts. How helpful is this? Massively!

Type options

Paragraph options

TYPE PREFERENCES SHORTCUT

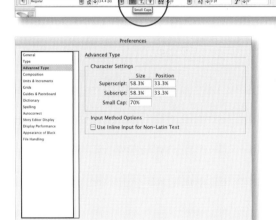

If you're using the Type tool and you want to get to the Type preferences fast, just Option-click (PC: Alt-click) on either the Superscript, Subscript, or Small Caps button up in the Control palette. This shortcut makes great sense, because in the Advanced Type Preferences dialog you can adjust the default Superscript, Subscript, and Small Cap settings.

   THE SECRET TO KERNING VISUALLY

Adjusting the space between two letters can certainly be done by going to the Character palette and manually entering numbers in the Kerning field, but that's so un-design-like. Good kerning is such a visual thing (and designers are such visual people) that entering numbers should be a last resort—we want to kern visually. Here's how it's done: Click your cursor between the two letters you want to kern, then press Option-Left Arrow (PC: Alt-Left Arrow) to kern (move) the letters closer together. Press Option-Right Arrow (PC: Alt-Right Arrow) to move them farther apart. Then, when it's time to kern another set of letters, use just the Left/Right Arrow keys to move your cursor to the letters, then add the Option key (PC: Alt key) to visually kern this set of letters.

   WHY ARE PARENTHESES IN MY KERNING FIELD?

That's InDesign's way of letting you know that the number you see in the field was generated by InDesign's Auto Kerning feature, which uses kerning pairs to adjust the space automatically between a pair of letters that are known to cause a spacing problem. You're welcome to change the kerning if it doesn't look right to you, but at least the parens let you know how (and why) that kerning value got there in the first place.

   TIGHTEN THE SPACE BETWEEN WORDS VISUALLY

When tracking words (adjusting the space between a number of selected letters or words), what exactly is the right amount? Nobody knows. That's because you have to do it visually, rather than numerically, to get it to look right. That's why it's so important to know this keyboard shortcut: Highlight the letters, or words, whose tracking you want to adjust, then press Option-Left Arrow (PC: Alt-Left Arrow) to tighten the spacing by moving the letters closer together or Option-Right Arrow (PC: Alt-Right Arrow) to move the letters farther apart.

ADJUST LEADING VISUALLY

Adjusting the vertical spacing between lines (known as leading) is another one of those adjustments that it's best to do visually rather than by the numbers. Just highlight the lines you want to adjust, then press Option-Up Arrow (PC: Alt-Up Arrow) to move the lines closer together, or Option-Down Arrow (PC: Alt-Down Arrow) to add more space between the lines.

    ADJUST HORIZONTAL SCALING VISUALLY

Want to make your type thinner or thicker without having to type values in the Horizontal Scale field in the Character palette? Try this: Switch to the Selection tool, select your text frame, hold the Command key (PC: Control key), grab one of the center points on the sides of your text frame, and drag inward to make the type thinner, or outward to make the letters wider (as shown below).

The 10 Legendary Warriors,

The 10 Legendary Warriors,

THE SPEED LANE TO 100% HORIZONTAL SCALING

As you know, we use horizontal scaling to make our letters thicker (like 120% or 130%) or thinner (I like to set all
my body copy at 95%), and since we're always tweaking
our horizontal scaling, wouldn't it be great if there was
a shortcut for a quick return to the standard 100%? Well
there is (you knew we were setting you up, right?). Just
press Shift-Command-X (PC: Shift-Control-X) and your
highlighted text will return to its good ol' default of
100% horizontal scaling.

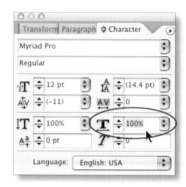

   DON'T KNOW THE RIGHT POINT SIZE? JUST DRAG YOUR TEXT

If you want to make your text much larger, but you're not sure which point size is right—
do it visually. Instead of highlighting the type and entering a number in the Font Size field,
get the Selection tool and click on the text block, hold Shift-Command (PC: Shift-Control),
grab a corner point of the text block and drag diagonally upward to enlarge it, or diagonally
inward to shrink it.

PROVEN STRENGTH

PROVEN STRENGTH

CHANGING MULTIPLE TEXT BLOCKS AT ONCE

If you want to change an attribute (like font, size, leading, etc.) in a number of text blocks at once, just get the Selection tool (the solid arrow), Shift-click on each text frame you want to adjust, switch to the Type tool, then go up to the Control palette and make your changes. Any changes you make will now be applied to all of the selected blocks of text.

 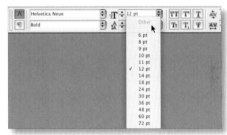

   APPLY CHARACTER FORMATTING TO MULTIPLE TEXT BLOCKS

This is one of our favorite InDesign tips, because it makes your type-tweaking life so much easier. If you have character formatting styles set up, you don't have to apply them one at a time. As in the previous tip, just get the Selection tool, Shift-click on every text block that you want to have a particular character formatting style, but this time go to the Character Styles palette or Paragraph Styles palette, click on the style, and BAM—they all change at once. Life is good.

 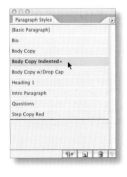

   ## SHORTCUT TO THE NEW CHARACTER STYLE DIALOG

Want a one-click way to get to the New Character Style dialog? Just go up in the Control palette and double-click the capital "A" that appears on the far right (just before the Character Styles pop-up menu) and the New Character Style dialog will pop right up.

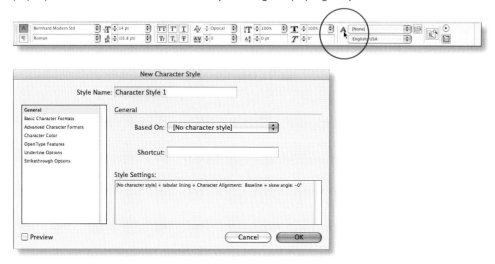

   ## SHIFT BASELINE WITHOUT THE CHARACTER PALETTE

Need to shift something up off the baseline (like the ® symbol) or move something down (like the 2 in H$_2$0)? You can do it using a keyboard shortcut: Highlight the character you want to shift, then press Shift-Option-Up Arrow (PC: Shift-Alt-Up Arrow) to move the character up, or Shift-Option-Down Arrow (PC: Shift-Alt-Down Arrow) to move the character down.

GET RID OF THOSE NASTY DOUBLE-SPACES

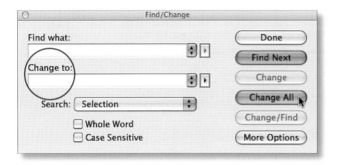

If you're importing text from a word processing document, there's a pretty good chance that the person who entered the text used the time-honored tradition of putting two spaces between sentences (a holdover from the days of using a typewriter). That's fine on a typewriter, with its monospace letters, but it looks terrible in today's typography and those double-spaces have to be removed. Here's how: Go under the Edit menu and choose Find/Change. Click in the Find What field, then press the Spacebar twice (you're telling it to find all double-spaces). Then tab to the Change To field and press the Spacebar once. Click the Change All button, and every double-space will instantly be changed to a single space. Pretty slick little trick, eh?

   GET RID OF WEIRD CHARACTERS

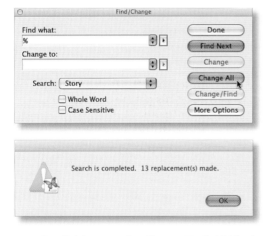

If you convert a QuarkXPress document into an InDesign document, you'll sometimes wind up with weird extra characters (like the % symbol appearing right in the middle of a word) throughout the document (at least, that usually happens to us). If so, you can have InDesign get rid of all of 'em, fast. Here's how: First select the weird character, then press Command-C (PC: Control-C) to copy it into memory. Then go under the Edit menu and choose Find/Change. When the dialog appears, click in the Find What field and then press Command-V (PC: Control-V) to paste the weird character into that field. Leave the Change To field blank, then click the Change All button. This then removes all the weird characters and replaces them with nothing. How sweet is that?

  FASTER FIXES FOR BAD CHARACTERS

In the previous tip, we showed you how to replace bad characters that appear when importing type or converting a QuarkXPress document to InDesign by using Find/Change under the Edit menu. Well, if you've had to replace those characters once, it's even faster the second time. Why? It's because InDesign remembers the last 15 finds and changes. So

if you convert a second document, you don't have to copy the offending bad character into the Find What field—instead just choose it from the field's pop-up menu, because it's already there. This can absolutely save loads of time when cleaning up a messy document.

   MAKE THAT SENTENCE ALL CAPS THE FAST WAY

If you've typed something, and then wish you'd entered it in all caps, you're only about three seconds away from having just that. Highlight the text you want in caps, and then press Shift-Command-K (PC: Shift-Control-K) and it's changed to all caps lickety-split.

The Standard of Luxury for New Car Owners

THE STANDARD OF LUXURY FOR NEW CAR OWNERS

HIGHLIGHT CHARACTER PALETTE FIELDS FAST

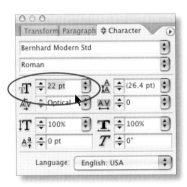

The next time you need to make a change in the Character palette, don't click your cursor in the tiny little field and then type in a new number—instead just click on the field's icon and the field will highlight, so all you have to do is type in the new amount. Sweet.

QUICK TYPE TWEAKING IN THE CHARACTER PALETTE

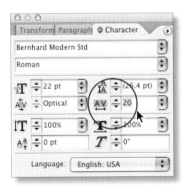

To keep working at maximum speed, we usually try to avoid using the Character palette as much as possible (having to type in values just takes too long), but if you have to work in the Character palette, here's a tip that speeds things up—as in the previous tip, when you want to adjust a value, just click on the icon for that field (to highlight the value already in that field), but instead of typing in a value, use the Up/Down Arrow keys on your keyboard to quickly increase or decrease the current amount. When you've got the number you want, press Enter.

FIND THE RIGHT FONT FAST—SCROLL THROUGH THEM

If you're not sure which font to use for a project, try this: Highlight the text in question, then just click your cursor once in the Font field (up in the Control palette, as shown here, or in the Character palette) and then use the Up/Down Arrow keys on your keyboard to move up and down the list of fonts. Each time you press an arrow key, the font will change to the next one in the list, which makes finding the right font a breeze.

   JUMP TO THE RIGHT FONT

If you know the name of the font you want, you don't have to scroll all the way through the font list to get to it. Just highlight the current font's name in the Font field (either in the Control palette or the Character palette) with your cursor, then type in the first letter of the font you want, and it will jump to that font. (Okay, technically it'll jump to the first font in the list that starts with that letter. So, if you have a lot of fonts, you might want to type in the first two or three letters, so it homes in on the exact font you want.)

CHANGE FONTS AUTOMATICALLY, WITHOUT STYLE SHEETS

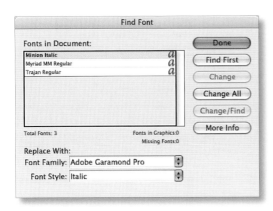

Let's say you have a multipage document, and all of the captions are in the font Minion Italic. If you used style sheets, you could change all the captions to a different face, say Adobe Garamond Pro Italic, very easily, but what if you didn't build style sheets (hey, it happens all the time)? Here's what to do: Go under the Type menu and choose Find Fonts. A list of the fonts used in your current document will appear in the window. Click on the font you want to replace (in this case, Minion Italic), then choose the Font Family and Font Style you want it replaced with from the pop-up menus at the bottom left of the dialog (in this case, Adobe Garamond Pro Italic). Click the Change All button, and all instances of Minion Italic in your document will be replaced with Adobe Garamond Pro Italic.

   PASTE TEXT INTO INDESIGN

If you're copying a small amount of text into your InDesign document, perhaps from a word processing program (such as Microsoft Word), probably the quickest way to do so is simply to highlight the text in your word processing program, press Command-C (PC: Control-C) to copy it, then switch to InDesign and press Command-V (PC: Control-V) to paste it in. If you can see your InDesign document onscreen, an even quicker way may be to click on the highlighted text in the word processing program and drag-and-drop it on the InDesign document.

PASTE TEXT WHILE RETAINING YOUR TYPE FORMATTING

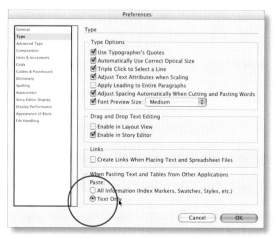

In previous versions of InDesign, if you pasted in text from another application, it kept the formatting of the original application. Personally, this drove me absolutely insane. In fact, it was the only thing about InDesign that I could say I really hated. But now, I can tell my therapist to cancel my standing Tuesday appointment because InDesign gives you the option to retain the formatting done in other applications, or to have your pasted text use the text formatting (font, size, leading, etc.) you're already using in InDesign. Just go to the InDesign menu (PC: Edit menu), under Preferences, choose Type, and in the When Pasting Text and Tables from Other Applications section, select Text Only. (Also, see "Paste Without Formatting" on page 239.)

   DRAG-AND-DROP TEXT INTO INDESIGN

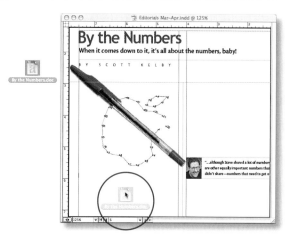

If you can see a text document on your desktop, you can actually drag-and-drop that text file from the desktop right into an open InDesign document, and the text will appear in its own text box. Weirder yet—it doesn't just work on text—try it on a graphic. That's right, it'll just drag-and-drop right on in.

GET CONTROL OVER YOUR IMPORTED TEXT

If you're importing text into InDesign, you can have a lot of control over how the text is imported by holding just one key. First, go under the File menu and choose Place. In the Place dialog, before you double-click on a text file to import it, just hold the Shift key, then double-click on it (or you can simply check Show Import Options). The Import Options dialog will appear, where you can control how your type will be imported and how certain aspects will be handled (like whether you want the quotes converted to typographer's quotes).

   HOW TO DESELECT EVERYTHING

If you have multiple items selected in InDesign, you may want to deselect—well—everything. If you're charging by the hour, go under the Edit menu and choose Deselect All. If you're charging by the job, just press Shift-Command-A (PC: Shift-Control-A).

ONE COLUMN TO MULTI-COLUMNS THE FAST WAY

If you've imported some text, you can instantly create multiple columns in that text by switching to the Selection tool (the black arrow on the left in the Toolbox), holding the Option key (PC: Alt key), and double-clicking on the text frame. This brings up the Text Frame Options dialog, and there you can choose how many columns you'd like your text split into. Turn on the Preview checkbox for a live preview of how your columns will look.

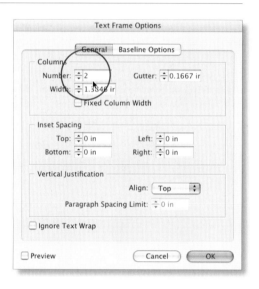

 ## NEED A ™? HOW ABOUT A ©?

Characters like ©, ™, and ® are called "special characters" and you can have InDesign insert these directly into your document. When you come to a situation that calls for a special character, just Control-click (PC: Right-click) right where your type cursor is and a pop-up menu will appear. Choose Insert Special Character from the pop-up menu and then choose which special character you want inserted from the submenu that appears (as shown here).

HOW TO USE GLYPHS

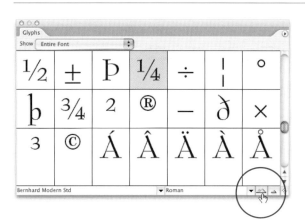

If you're reading this tip, and you're into typography, you already know that many fonts have glyphs (extra characters used in professional typesetting, like real fractions, alternate letters, swash letters, etc.). Well, you can find a font's glyphs and insert them directly by going under the Type menu and choosing Glyphs to bring up the Glyphs palette. From there, you can see all the alternate letters for the currently selected typeface, and if you want to insert one of those characters into your document, just double-click directly on the box that contains that character.

   GLYPH CHARACTERS TOO SMALL? HEAD FOR THE MOUNTAINS

If the default size of the alternate characters in the Glyphs palette appears too small (and it is), just click on the left mountain button at the bottom of the palette and the characters will jump up to the next size. Click it again, they get even larger. To make the glyphs smaller, just click on the right mountain button. So give these mountains a couple of good clicks and this palette will be much easier to use.

FIVE KEY SHORTCUTS FOR SELECTING TEXT

If you find yourself working a lot with type (especially if you're editing text), you can save loads of time by learning a few simple shortcuts for selecting type. For example:

1. To select an entire word, just double-click on it.
2. To select characters to the left of where your text cursor is located, just press Shift-Left Arrow. To select characters to the right, press (duh) Shift-Right Arrow. Each time you press the Shift-Arrow keys, it adds more characters to the selection.
3. To select a whole line of text, triple-click on it.
4. To select an entire paragraph, quadruple-click (it's easier than it sounds).
5. And last, Shift-Command-\ (PC: Shift-Control-\) selects the line where your text cursor is.

Use these five simple shortcuts, and you'll save more time every day than you'd ever imagine.

   EDIT WHILE YOU CHECK SPELLING

The spelling checker may look like a dialog, but if you give it a closer look you'll find it's actually a floating palette. How is that different? Well, since it's a floating palette, you can be in the middle of a spell-check, leave the palette, make an adjustment to your document, and then go back to the Check Spelling palette and pick right up where you left off. We usually wind up doing this when we accidentally click the Ignore button—and right when we do, we realize we missed a misspelled word; so we leave the palette, manually type the correct spelling right into the document, then we return to the Check Spelling palette and finish the job.

SAVE TIME WHEN CHECKING SPELLING

Like most spelling checkers, InDesign's checker lets you add words it doesn't recognize during the spell-checking process (words like your name or your company's name), but you'll save time if rather than waiting until these names come up during a spell-check, you enter them now, in the InDesign Dictionary. Go under the Edit menu, under Spelling, and choose Dictionary. This brings up a dialog where you can enter your name, your company's name, and other words that the built-in dictionary just won't recognize.

 VOILÀ! THE TRICK TO SPELL-CHECKING FOREIGN LANGUAGES

InDesign comes with a number of international dictionaries built right in, so if you're like Frasier and like to work as many French words and phrases as possible into everyday language, at least now you can make sure they're spelled right. Just highlight the French (German, Italian, Spanish, etc.) word you want to check, then go to the Character palette and at the bottom you'll see a pop-up list of languages (if you don't see this pop-up list, it means your Character palette's options are hidden, so just go to the palette's flyout menu and choose Show Options). The language is set to English: USA by default (at least ours is) so change it to French, which loads the French dictionary. Now you can use the Check Spelling palette (under the Edit menu, choose Spelling, and then Check Spelling) just like always, but now it'll check your French words. C'est magnifique!

HOW TO STOP A WORD FROM BEING HYPHENATED

If you have a word that you never want to be hyphenated (some words like "inappropriate" or "invisible" generally shouldn't be hyphenated, because in these usages the prefix "in" stands for "not"), you can let InDesign know that's what you want by entering the word into the Dictionary (found under the Edit menu, under the Spelling menu) with a ~ (tilde) before the word and clicking the Add button. Once it sees that, it won't hyphenate that word.

 IT'S OKAY TO USE THE BOLD SHORTCUT

Back in the olden days of digital layout programs, if you highlighted some text, then used the keyboard shortcut for bold, it looked for a bold version of your current font. If it didn't find a bold version, it would fake it. This usually looked horrible, but most people were working on pretty awful non-PostScript printers, so really—who cared? Worse than that, sometimes it looked bold onscreen, but that bolding went away when you printed the document. But InDesign is smarter than that. If you highlight some text and press the international standard for bold text: Shift-Command-B (PC: Shift-Control-B), InDesign will apply the next heaviest weight of your typeface. If there is no bold version of your current font, it will (get this) just ignore it. So basically, you're safe to use the shortcut—it won't burn you like it did in the old days. Same thing for italics: Press Shift-Command-I (PC: Shift-Control-I); if there's not an italic version, it'll just ignore it, but best of all, it won't show a fake italic onscreen.

WHEN FONTS COLLIDE (HOW TO ADD LIGATURES)

Certain lowercase letters, because of their design, collide (touch) when you use them side by side, such as the lowercase "f" and "i" in the word "fi-nally." Typographers feel that collision looks really bad. It looks "inelegant" (if that's actually a word), so the type designers invented ligatures. Ligatures are custom-made combinations of two normally colliding characters that have been engineered into one beautiful character. They're designed to touch, but in an elegant way. Today, most professional quality typefaces include a set of ligatures; you just have to activate them by going to the Character palette's flyout menu and choosing Ligatures. It then looks for instances of lowercase letter combinations (like fi or fl) and converts them on the fly. If you want your type to look its best, you'll definitely want to start using ligatures.

finally
finally

   SET TYPE JUSTIFICATION THE FAST WAY

You don't have to head to the Paragraph palette or Control palette to set your type as left justified, right justified, or centered because the keyboard shortcuts all use the first letter of the justification style. For example, for left justification use Shift-Command-L (PC: Shift-Control-L) and the "L" is for left. We're not going to embarrass you by telling you the other two—they're pretty obvious.

Justify Left | Justify Center | Justify Right

INDENT PARAGRAPHS (HOW AND HOW MUCH)

We use indents to tell the reader "Here's a new paragraph," and creating these indents is easy—just open the Paragraph palette (opening the Character palette will usually get you one click from the Paragraph palette, because they're nested together by default), then in the second field from the top, enter the amount you want for your indent. So, how much should you indent? It's up to you, but many professionals agree that the exact proper amount is the width of a capital "M" in the typeface you're using. (For example, the typeface we're using here is Myriad, and in that face an indent of .10 is approxi-

mately equal to one capital letter M. Now, personally, we think .10 isn't enough indent so we generally use a .15-inch indent for most of our standard body copy regardless of the typeface; but hey, that's just us.)

   DOING A PULL QUOTE?
BETTER HANG THOSE QUOTE MARKS, BUNKY

If you're pulling a quote out of some text (this is hugely popular in magazines), then you're going to have quotes around the text, right? Well, if you do this, the pros always (always) "hang" their punctuation. By hanging, we mean the opening quote literally hangs outside the text block to the left, as if it started one character before the actual text begins (you can see an example here).

> "You're a little confused. If the bugs didn't hide, I wouldn't have to find them."
>
> *The opening quote needs to be hung*

> "You're a little confused. If the bugs didn't hide, I wouldn't have to find them."
>
> *Here's the quote hung*

How important is hanging your quotes? Adobe made a separate palette just for it—the Story palette, which is found under the Type menu. When the palette appears (shown here), turn on the checkbox for Optical Margin Alignment, then enter the point size of your type, so it properly aligns your quotes. That's it, bunky.

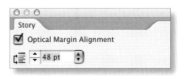

ADD DROP SHADOWS TO TEXT

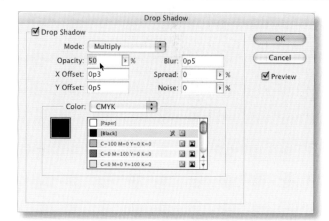

Want to add a drop shadow to your text? (If you do, make sure it's large display-sized text—something like 36 points or larger.) Select your text block with the Selection tool, then go under the Object menu and choose Drop Shadow. When the Drop Shadow dialog appears (by default it's turned off— I know, that doesn't make sense), you have to turn it on by clicking on the Drop Shadow checkbox at the top left corner of the dialog. Then you'll also want to turn on the Preview checkbox (it's off by default—don't get me started) so you can actually see what the shadow looks like before you click OK.

MAKE YOUR TEXT FRAME FIT THE TEXT

If you've been using InDesign for a while (before the CS version), you are going to lose your mind with this little improvement. You know how you drag out a text frame, then you start typing in your text, but the text frame is always WAY bigger than the text, so if you want it to fit snugly, you have to resize the frame manually? Not anymore. Thankfully, Adobe felt your pain and now to fit your text frame snugly around your text, just switch to the Selection tool, go up to the Control palette, and click on the Fit Frame to Content button and suddenly your whole world makes sense.

HOW TO MOVE OBJECTS WHILE YOUR TEXT IS SELECTED

Okay, this may sound a bit esoteric, but it's more useful than you'd think. Here's a typical scenario: You highlight some text to adjust it, you start increasing the size of the text, and it starts to overlap another object on the page (a photo, a box, a graphic—whatever). So you have to switch to the Selection tool, move the object out of the way, and then switch back to the Type tool and re-highlight your text. A pain, right? Right. But instead, even while your text is highlighted, you can hold the Command key (PC: Control key) to switch temporarily to a mini-Selection tool so you can reposition the object while your text remains highlighted. Release the Command key (PC: Control key) and you're back to your Type tool, saving loads of time and aggravation. This is only one scenario where you'll use this—believe me, you'll find a dozen more.

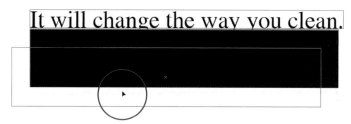

   GET LIVE TEXT WRAP PREVIEWS WHILE YOU MOVE

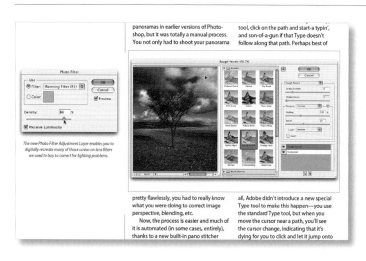

If you've applied text wrap to a graphic, and you move the graphic, it waits until you release the mouse button to "re-wrap." But if you'd like to see a live text wrap while you move your graphic, just click on the graphic and hold a moment before you drag; then when you drag, the text will re-wrap in real time as you move.

APPLY GRADIENTS TO EDITABLE TYPE

InDesign is one of the few programs out there that will let you apply a gradient to type and have that type still editable (most require that you convert your type into a graphic before you apply a gradient; and once it's converted you can no longer change the font, leading, spacing, etc.). To do this "live type gradient," you just set your type, click on the text frame with the Selection tool to select it, then in the Toolbox click the Formatting Affects Text icon (the "T" just below the Fill/Stroke swatches). Now open the Gradient palette (it's found under the Window menu), create the gradient you want, and your type will be filled with that gradient.

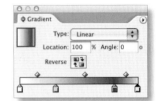

   FASTER TEXT FRAME MOVING

If you're adjusting your layout, when it comes to moving your text frames around, it's good to know this little tip: If you click, hold, and drag a text frame, you'll see the text displayed as you drag; and because InDesign is rendering this text live as you drag, it moves slower. However, if you want to reposition text frames as fast as possible, don't click, hold, and drag—just click and immediately drag. Then InDesign only displays a "ghost" of the frame (the outline with no contents, shown here with a blue outline) and it moves at full speed.

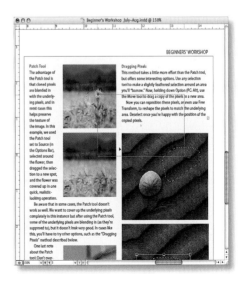

GET THE GRABBER WHEN YOU'VE GOT THE TYPE TOOL

When you're working with any tool except the Type tool, you press the Spacebar to get the Hand tool (which you click-and-drag to move around your document), but when you have the Type tool there's a different shortcut—instead hold the Option key (PC: Alt key) when you have a text insertion point, and your Type tool will temporarily change into the Hand tool.

Super Slam Saturday

CHOOSE CUSTOM FONTS AND SIZES IN STORY EDITOR

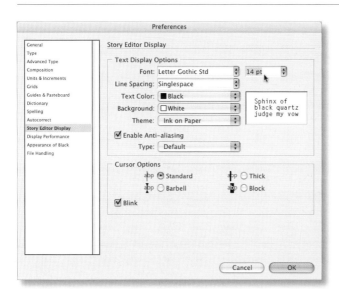

If you're using the Story Editor feature in InDesign (which means you're secretly an old PageMaker freak), then you'll be happy to know you have some control over the font and size of the Story Editor text display. Just go under the InDesign menu (PC: Edit menu), under Preferences, under Story Editor Display, and you'll find a host of controls, including font, font size, and even what your cursor looks like while you're in the Story Editor.

ACCESS MASTER PAGE TEXT FRAMES ON A REGULAR PAGE

If you set up text frames on a master page in your document, those frames aren't accessible within a regular page. That is, unless you know this trick—just Shift-Command-click (PC: Shift-Control-click) on the text frame. This overrides the master page, so that frame is made active (as shown here), and a text frame placed on the master page becomes editable on a regular page.

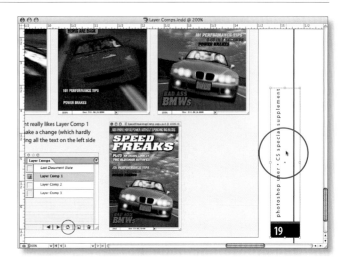

   USE THE RIGHT DASH

Okay, if you're using InDesign, you're no longer typing on your computer. Now you're "setting type." Since you don't want it to be a dead giveaway that you're not a professional typographer, you'll need to use the right dashes—typographer's dashes (in other words, you'll only use hyphens to hyphenate words and that's it). For example, to express time (like "the party is from 8:00 p.m.–10:00 p.m.") you use an "en" dash, which is longer than a regular dash (or hyphen). You get an en dash by pressing Option-Hyphen (PC: Alt-Hyphen). When you've got an abrupt change in thought, but you don't want to end the sentence or use a comma, use an "em" dash, which is a really long dash—like that one there (usually used without a space—right up against the next letter). To get an em dash press Shift-Option-Hyphen (PC: Shift-Alt-Hyphen).

> Using a Hyphen
> The party is from 8:00 p.m.-10:00 p.m.
>
> Using an En Dash
> The party is from 8:00 p.m.–10:00 p.m.

NOT JUST A SPACE. A "SPECIAL" SPACE

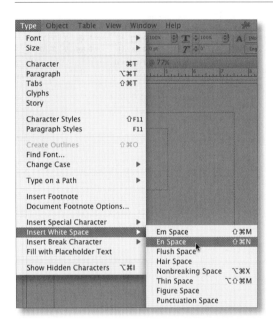

When you're working with type, sometimes a regular old Spacebar space is too big. Sometimes you need something less. A mini-space, if you will. Well, InDesign is chock-full of freaky, I mean "professional," spaces. You find them by going under the Type menu, under Insert White Space, and you'll find a whole submenu of spaces, including popular typographer's spaces like en and em spaces. My favorite is Hair Space. I have no earthly idea what it is, but I just like the name. (Okay, I do know—a hair space is just what it sounds like it would be: a really, really thin space that is $1/24$ the width of an em space. Ants use these fairly often.)

Color
Blind

WORKING
WITH COLOR

Now why would anyone title a chapter about working with color "Color Blind"? Well, here's the thing. It's always been our credo (by the way, I have no idea what a

Color Blind
working with color

credo is) to title our chapters with the name of a song or a movie, and then below the title, the real description of the chapter appears as a subhead. Is this a good plan? No. But it's what we do (it's that credo thing again). So, is there a song named "Color Blind"? Yup (it's by Michael W. Smith). I originally wanted to use Color Me Badd, which was the name of a group that had some hits back in the 80s (remember "I want to sex you up"?), but I didn't think Color Me Badd sounded positive enough. Color Me Good has a better feeling, but I couldn't find a band named Color Me Good; so Color Blind, while not a stellar chapter name, won the nod. By the way, there's also a song named "Color Blind Dog" by Dishpan, and I briefly considered that as well, but I hate chapter names that make you feel sad (e.g., "That poor little dog," etc.).

   DRAG FROM PALETTE TO PALETTE

Here's a nice time saver—if you've created a color in the Color palette, the quickest way to save that color to your Swatches palette is to just drag-and-drop it. Just click directly on the preview swatch in the Color palette, and drag that over to the Swatches palette. Again, you'll see the cursor change to a hand with a plus (+) sign, and a black horizontal line will appear in the Swatches palette right where your swatch will appear—all you have to do is let go of the mouse button and that custom color will now be saved as a color swatch in your Swatches palette.

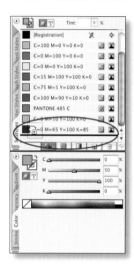

   CREATE YOUR GRADIENTS WITH DRAG-AND-DROP

InDesign has a way to create your gradients—drag-and-drop. That's right, just grab a color swatch from the Swatches palette and drag it right onto a Color Stop in the Gradients palette and the stop takes on that color. Freaky!

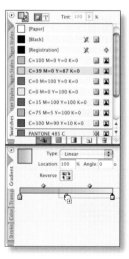

CREATE A DEFAULT SET OF COLORS

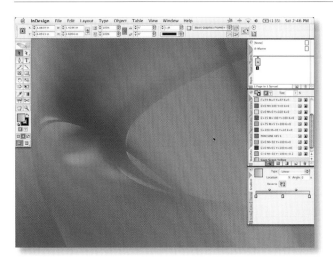

If you'd like a special set of custom colors to appear as your default colors (so every time you open a new document, those colors are already in place), it's fairly simple. Just close any open documents, then go to the Color palette, create your new colors, drag-and-drop them to the Swatches palette and you're done! The next time you open a new document (and for all future documents), these new custom colors are set as the default swatches.

   STEAL COLORS FROM ANOTHER DOCUMENT

If you've taken the time to create some custom colors in one document, you can steal those colors, all at once, and move them into your new document. Here's how: Just go to the Swatches palette and from its flyout menu choose Load Swatches. When the Open A File dialog appears, navigate to the document you want to steal colors from, then click Open, and the swatches from that document will load into your currently open Swatches palette.

   NOT JUST FOR TEXT STYLE SHEETS—BUT COLOR STYLE SHEETS TOO

If you've painstakingly created a custom fill and stroke pattern for an object, and later on you want to apply those exact same specs to another object, you don't have to rebuild it all from scratch. Start by clicking on the new object, then get the Eyedropper tool and click on the object whose attributes (fill, stroke width, color, etc.) you want to steal. When you click, all

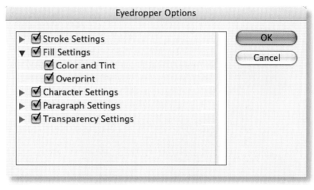

those attributes will be applied to your new object. How do you control how many attributes the Eyedropper picks up? Just go to the Toolbox, double-click on the Eyedropper, and an Eyedropper Options dialog will appear (shown here) where you can choose which attributes it copies and which it ignores.

   EYEDROPPER TRICK #2

Okay, so you've applied the attributes of one object to another—now how do you sample a different object? If you click on it with the Eyedropper tool, it'll change to the attributes of the first object that you sampled from. Do you

have to first switch to the Selection tool? Nope. While you have the Eyedropper tool, just hold the Option key (PC: Alt key) and then click on the new object, and rather than filling, it will sample those attributes of the second object.

  ## SAVE TIME BY DRAGGING AND DROPPING COLOR

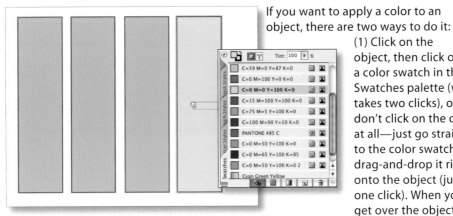

If you want to apply a color to an object, there are two ways to do it: (1) Click on the object, then click on a color swatch in the Swatches palette (which takes two clicks), or (2) don't click on the object at all—just go straight to the color swatch and drag-and-drop it right onto the object (just one click). When you get over the object you want to drop a color onto, the cursor will change to a hand with a plus (+) sign, so you know it has recognized that you're dragging and dropping color. This is a big time saver and as many times as we apply color, it can save you hundreds of clicks in no time.

   ## DELETE MULTIPLE SWATCHES

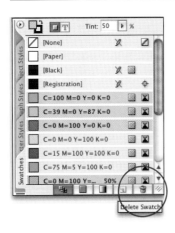

To delete multiple swatches from the Swatches palette, just hold the Command key (PC: Control key), click on all the swatches you want to delete (which selects them), then just click once on the Trash icon at the bottom of the Swatches palette.

IF YOU DIDN'T USE IT, LOSE IT

When you want to send your document to a printer or service provider, you should make the document as simple as possible to alleviate any potential doubt or confusion as to what you did. Therefore, you should delete any unused color swatches from the Swatches palette so that your printer will know exactly which colors are used in the document. InDesign has no single command to do this, but you can do it in two steps. Choose Select All Unused from the Swatches palette's flyout menu. This will highlight all your unused swatches, then just click the Trash icon at the bottom of the Swatches palette to delete them all in one click.

   MERGE SWATCHES

An alternative way to delete swatches is to simply merge the swatches you don't want into one swatch you do want. Here's how: Start by clicking on the swatch you want to keep, then Command-click (PC: Control-click) on the swatches you want to delete. Now, to merge them go to the palette's flyout menu and choose Merge Swatches. All that will be left is the first swatch you clicked on (the one you wanted to keep) and the others are long gone!

CHANGE THE ORDER OF YOUR SWATCHES

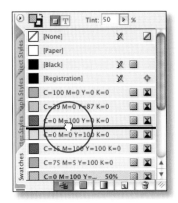

If you're familiar with Photoshop's Layers palette, you'll have no problem rearranging InDesign's color swatches because they work in a very similar manner. Just click on the swatch you want to move, and drag it up (or down) the Swatches palette to the location where you want it.

   ## SAVE TINTS AS SWATCHES

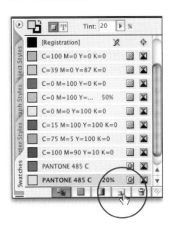

Creating a tint of the color currently selected in the Swatches palette is easy; just move the Tint slider at the top of the palette from 100% to a lower number. However, once you raise that Tint slider back up to 100% (perhaps you're now working on a different swatch), your tint is now long gone. To avoid that, you have to save your custom tint as a swatch—first click on the color you want to use as the tint base. Then use the Tint slider to create the tint you want. Once the tint looks right, click the New Swatch icon at the bottom of the Swatches palette and that tint is now saved as a totally separate color. Changes you make in the Color palette will no longer affect your tint because now it is saved as its own separate swatch.

CHAPTER 3 • Working with Color   **65**

AVOID TINT WEIRDNESS

InDesign handles tints differently than you might think, and that's why we included this tip to keep you from experiencing tint "weirdness." The Tint control in the Swatches palette is really a "master" Tint slider because it applies the tint percentage to every swatch you click on. So if you click on one swatch, and lower the tint of that swatch to 62%, then you click on another swatch, that swatch also becomes a 62% tint. If you raise it back to 100%, you also just raised the previous swatch (the one you originally set to 62%) back to 100%. In fact, if you save a 52% tint as a swatch, and if you even as much as click on that swatch, it moves the master Tint slider to 52% for all your swatches. Yes, it's weird, but we thought you should know.

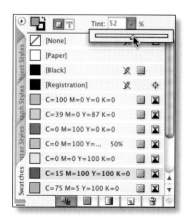

   TINT WEIRDNESS #2

Just when you thought it couldn't get any weirder, there's this: Let's say you clicked on a purple swatch, lowered the tint to 40%, then saved it as its own separate swatch (so the Tint slider would no longer affect it). Then you did the same thing again for tints that are 20% and 30%. If you were to edit your purple swatch (let's say you added more red) it would automatically affect (or update, if you will) all your other tints. They're somehow tied to the "mother swatch." This can either be a cool feature or an annoying bug—it just depends on how you look at it.

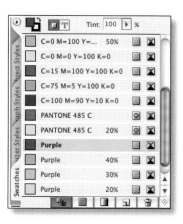

NAME COLOR SWATCHES AFTER THEIR VALUES

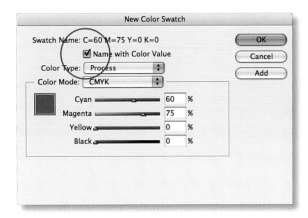

Do you ever get tired of trying to figure out or remember what colors you used in a previous layout? Are you trying to re-create that same shade of blue that worked so well for you last year? When you create a new process swatch in the New Color Swatch dialog, the box labeled Name with Color Value is turned on by default. This automatically names your swatch with the values of cyan, magenta, yellow, and black that you've used. It will also update if you go back later and change your mind.

HOW TO NAME SWATCHES (AND WHY YOU SHOULD)

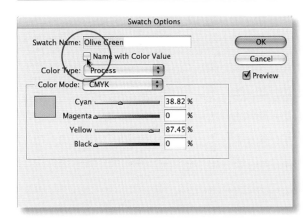

As mentioned in the previous tip, when you create a new color swatch, by default it's named using the build of the color (i.e., C=39, M=0, Y=87, K=0). Unless you're a prepress operator, it's not the most descriptive name. To rename it with a "human" name (like "Olive Green" or "Frank"), go to the Swatches palette and double-click directly on the swatch. That'll bring up the Swatch Options dialog. The Swatch Name field is not acces-

sible until you turn off the Name with Color Value checkbox. Then a field appears where you can name the swatch. Besides sheer ease of use, if you're using spot color on a printing press, there's another reason to rename your swatches—so the pressman can figure out which colors to put on press, because spot colors aren't color builds like process colors.

LOAD THE PANTONE COLORS

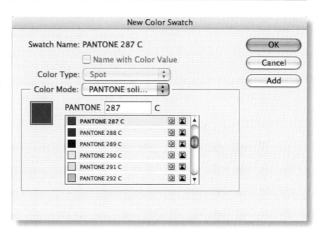

If you've been wondering where the Pantone colors are hiding, we can help. Go to the Swatches palette and from its flyout menu choose New Color Swatch. A New Color Swatch dialog will appear (shown here) and if you click on the Color Mode pop-up menu, you'll see a list of all the color libraries, which are installed with InDesign. Choose the one you want (in this case, PANTONE solid coated) and that set immediately loads. To choose a particular color, type the number in the PANTONE field.

   IMPORT JUST A FEW, OR ALL, OF THE PANTONE COLORS

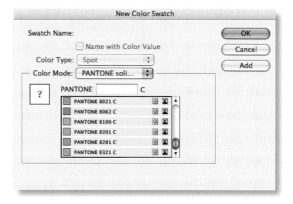

In the previous tip we showed you how to choose an individual Pantone color as your color swatch, but what if you want to import seven or eight Pantone swatches? What if you want to import them all? Here's how: To import multiple Pantone colors, go to the Swatches palette and choose New Color Swatch from the palette's flyout menu. Then from the Color Mode pop-up menu choose which Pantone color set you want. That set will load, and they will be displayed as a list in the dialog. Command-click (PC: Control-click) on the individual Pantone swatches you want to import, then click the Add button. If you want to import the entire Pantone set into your Swatches palette, click on the first visible Pantone swatch, then scroll to the bottom of the list, hold the Shift key and click on the last swatch, then click OK, and all the Pantone swatches in that set will load into your Swatches palette, where you'll spend the rest of your natural life scrolling through the hundreds of swatches.

SPEED THROUGH THE SWATCHES PALETTE

Want to get to a particular color in your Swatches palette in a hurry? Hold Option-Command (PC: Alt-Control) and click within your Swatches palette (you'll see a thin black highlight line appear around the list area of your Swatches palette). Now you can simply type in the first letter (or first few letters) of the name of the color swatch you want and it'll jump right to that swatch (this is yet another reason why you want to name your color swatches). This is particularly helpful if you've loaded an entire Pantone set.

THE SMART WAY TO EDIT SWATCHES

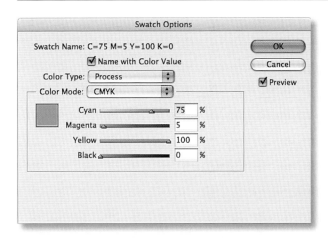

If you have objects selected in your document, you have to be careful about editing color swatches. If you simply head over to the Swatches palette and double-click on a swatch to edit it, in the split second before the Swatch Options dialog appears, all your selected objects will change to that color. But you can get around that with this important tip—before you double-click on a swatch, hold Shift-Option-Command (PC: Shift-Alt-Control). Then you can double-click on any swatch, edit the color, and not worry about affecting any selected object. (Of course, if you edit the color swatch for the selected objects, those objects will change color when you click OK, but you knew that, right?)

SPEED THROUGH THE COLOR RAMP

When you're using the Color palette, there's a ramp (spectrum) at the bottom of the palette where you can click directly on any color within the currently selected color model (RGB, LAB, or CMYK). You change which color model is selected by choosing it from the palette's flyout menu, but there's an even faster way—just Shift-click anywhere in the ramp, and the next color model will appear in the ramp.

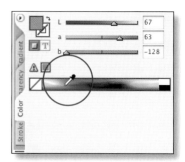

 GET SOLID BLACK, OR SOLID WHITE, IN ONE CLICK

I know a lot of longtime users who didn't realize that if you're looking for solid white or solid black, there's a shortcut that will keep you moving at full speed. At the bottom of the Color palette is a color spectrum, and at the end of this spectrum are two swatches: one white, one black. If you need either color, go right there and you're one click away.

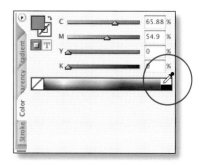

GET YOUR COLORS IN GAMUT WITH ONE CLICK

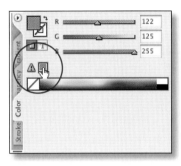

If you create a color that is out of the CMYK printing gamut (out of range of what a CMYK printing press can print), you'll see a little yellow warning symbol (shown here) appear just above the color spectrum in the Color palette. So the warning tells you it's out of gamut, but how do you get that color in gamut? Just click directly on the warning symbol, and it will give you the closest in-gamut color available.

   CREATE PERFECT SHADES

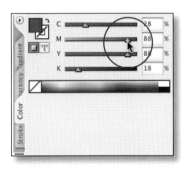

If you've created a color (using the Color palette, of course) and then you decide you want to see a lighter shade of that same color, here's a trick you'll love—just hold the Shift key, grab one of the color sliders (as shown here) and all the other sliders will move right along with it, giving you either a lighter shade (if you drag left with CMYK; right with RGB) or a more saturated version of the color (if you drag right with CMYK; left with RGB).

GET THE COLOR PALETTE INTO TINT MODE

Want to get the Color palette into tint mode fast (where it gives you the 100% to 0% Tint slider)? Just click on any swatch in the Swatches palette and the Color palette then switches immediately to tint mode (as shown here).

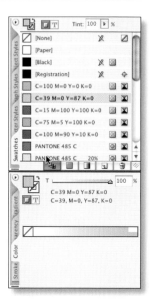

   ## HELP WITH CREATING COLORS

Not sure which colors to mix to create an olive color? Look to the sliders, Luke. If you look in the Color palette, the sliders appear in color. That's not just for looks—those sliders show you exactly where to drag to get the color you want. If you're in CMYK and the sliders look black, lower the black amount until you can start to see some color. If you don't see olive there, drag the top slider to the left and look at the color sliders—is it closer or farther away from olive? In just a few seconds of experimenting, you'll probably see just which sliders you need to drag where. (Here's a hint—to get to olive, start with just the green slider, then add a little red.)

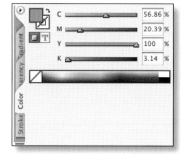

ONE CLICK TO NO FILL OR STROKE

Want to quickly set your current fill (or stroke) to None? Save yourself a trip to the Toolbox and just press the "/" (slash) key.

   SWAP THE FILL AND STROKE

If you've been adjusting the stroke color and decide now you want to swap the fill color and the stroke color, you could of course head over to the Toolbox and click the Swap Fill and Stroke icon, or you could use this handy shortcut—Shift-X and it'll do it for you.

RETURN TO THE DEFAULT BLACK STROKE, NO FILL

The default settings for InDesign's stroke and fill are black for the stroke, and no fill (so if you were to draw a box, it would be empty in the middle, with a thin black stroke around it). To get back to these default settings anytime, press the same key as Photoshop uses to reset its default Foreground/Background colors—the letter "d." Of course, you could click the little Default Fill and Stroke icon (circled here) to return to the default colors, but who has time for that, eh?

 DRAG-AND-DROP COLORS FROM THE TOOLBOX

Earlier we talked about how you can drag-and-drop color from the Swatches palette onto an object within your document; but you can do the exact same thing from the Toolbox—if you want to apply the current selected fill or stroke color, just click on the Fill or Stroke thumbnail and drag-and-drop it right where you want it.

GET LIVE GRADIENT PREVIEWS

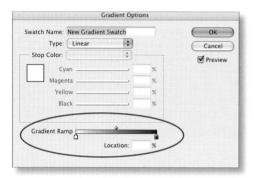

If you're creating a gradient to apply to an object (or text), once you've applied the gradient, you can adjust the gradient ramp and see how the adjustments will affect the selected object live, in real time. Here's how: Just click on the object that has the gradient applied, then go to the Swatches palette where you'll see your gradient selected. Double-click on it, and the Gradient Options dialog will appear (as shown here). At the bottom of the dialog is a Gradient Ramp with all your color stops. If you click the Preview button (it's off by default) the changes you make in this Gradient Ramp are updated live onscreen, saving you from having to guess how your changes will affect your object.

   REAPPLY THE LAST-USED GRADIENT

If you recently applied a gradient, you can reapply that same gradient by selecting an object and just pressing the period (.) key. (That's a shortcut that keeps you from going to the bottom of the Toolbox and hitting the Apply Gradient icon shown here, which also applies the last gradient used.)

   COLOR MANAGEMENT WHEN IMPORTING PHOTOS

If you've set up a color management system within Adobe Photoshop, InDesign can take advantage of it, including reading embedded color profiles of imported images and assigning color profiles. In InDesign CS2, color management is on by default. Go to Edit>Color Settings. From there, you can control how your images are color managed. What does that mean? That's a whole book unto itself. Check out Bruce Fraser, Fred Bunting, and Chris Murphy's *Real World Color Management* from Peachpit Press.

   GRADIENT PALETTE SHORTCUT

Here's a quick way to get the Gradient palette open—just double-click on the Gradient tool in the Toolbox and it will pop right up.

MAKE SURE ALL THE COLORS IN YOUR BOOK MATCH

If you're creating a book, magazine, or other project that uses multiple documents, it's important that all your color swatches match exactly (in other words, you don't want one version of red in one section, and then a slightly different shade in another). Well, InDesign lets you make sure all your colors match exactly by syncing all the swatches in your separate documents together, so they're all using the exact same "red." Here's how: Go under the File menu, under New, and choose Book. Save your book (which brings up the Book palette), then press the +

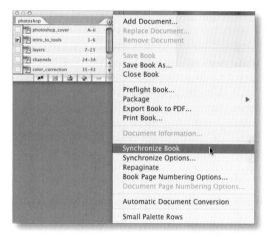

sign at the bottom of the palette to add the chapters you want sync'd together. Once you have all the chapters in your Book palette, choose Synchronize Book from the palette's flyout menu. By default, it not only syncs your color swatches, but it syncs your Character Styles and Paragraph Styles as well. (If you want to sync only your color swatches, choose Synchronize Options from the flyout menu and turn off the checkboxes for Character Styles and Paragraph Styles.)

   BLUE AND YELLOW MAKE GREEN

Takes you back to your elementary school days, doesn't it? Rather than getting out the finger paints, overlap two objects of different colors. Bring up the Attributes palette from the Window menu. Select just the top object and check the Overprint Fill box. When your document prints, the color on top will be mixed with the color below.

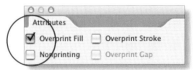

   STOP PLAYING HIT-OR-MISS

Overprinting doesn't have to be a guessing game. Nor do you have to keep wasting color ink and paper. If you have objects set to overprint, simply choose Overprint Preview from the View menu to see exactly how those inks will be mixed together.

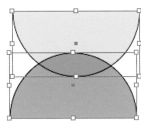

Drawing Fire

DRAWING WITH INDESIGN

I know what you're thinking: "I didn't know you could draw with InDesign." Nobody does. Well, somebody does, but he's not talkin'. Actually, InDesign has a number

Drawing Fire

drawing with InDesign

of shape tools and a Pen tool, so you can draw quite a few things. Of course—it really helps if you know how to draw. If not, you'll wind up with a bunch of polygons, rectangles, circles, and the occasional oval. So, if you can't draw, should you still read this chapter? No. Don't read it.

Skip immediately to the next chapter and pretend this one doesn't exist. It's not for you. It's not intended for your viewing, so please do us all a favor and just move on before you create a scene. Now, why would we tell you not to read this chapter? To hook you. Now that we've told you not to read this chapter, you're definitely going to read it. You're dying to read it. It's killing you that there might be things in here, naughty things, that you're not supposed to read, so even though you can't draw as much as a stick-man, you're going to read every single line, every page, and drink it all up because you know there's more to this chapter than we're letting on. See, you're smarter than we thought.

EDIT ONE OBJECT IN A GROUP

If you've grouped some objects together and you need to scale (or edit) only one of them, just get the Direct Selection tool (the hollow arrow) and click on the object you want to edit; that one object will be selected, rather than the entire group. In the example shown here, we selected one circle within the grouped image, changed the color, and increased its size.

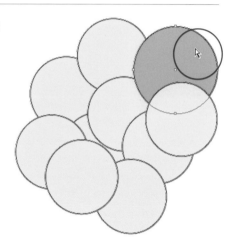

 TURN YOUR FONT INTO A GRAPHIC

Want to do some freaky things to your type? Then you'll have to convert it from type into a graphic—and at that point, the rules of typography go out the window. You can stretch, squeeze, distort, and torment your type just as you would any other graphic object. To do this, select your text, then go under the Type menu and choose Create Outlines. This changes your type into paths (as if you had drawn each letter manually with the Pen

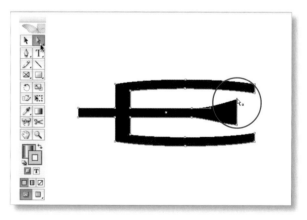

tool); because it now has paths, you can use the Direct Selection tool (as shown here) to grab points and extend them (for creating custom type logos) or use the Pen tool to add, subtract, and otherwise edit its anchor points.

SMOOTH OUT THOSE JAGGY PATHS

Got a jaggy path? (It happens all the time, especially if you're drawing your paths with a mouse instead of a Wacom graphics tablet.) The problem is usually caused by having too many points (which makes things look jaggy, rather than nice and smooth). Well, you can fix those jaggy paths with the seldom-used (but very powerful) Smooth tool. Get the Smooth tool from the Toolbox (it's under the Pencil tool—which is probably why nobody's found it) and just trace over areas of your path that have too many points. It removes any extraneous anchor points while trying to keep your original shape as intact as possible. Try it once and you'll see what we mean. It's smooooooth!

   ADD SOFT EDGES TO OBJECTS

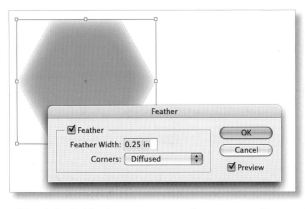

If you want to add a soft edge effect to an object, just Control-click (PC: Right-click) on the object and choose Feather from the pop-up menu that appears. This brings up the Feather dialog (shown here), where you can enter the amount of feathering you'd like (the higher the number, the softer the edges of your selected object will appear). Also, the Preview checkbox is off by default (don't get me started), so to actually see what's happening as you apply the feathering, click this Preview checkbox.

BACKSCREENING EFFECTS

If you want to put text that is easily seen over a photo in InDesign, then you'll want to know this backscreening trick. Just use the Rectangle tool to draw a rectangle over the area of the photo where you want text to appear. Fill this rectangle with white (or paper) from the Swatches palette, then go under the Window menu and choose Transparency

to bring up that palette. Lower the opacity (as shown here) so you can see the photo behind the box. Now you can add your text and it will be easily seen over the photo.

   HOW MANY SIDES WITH THAT POLYGON?

If you want to specify how many sides your polygon will have before you draw it, just double-click the Polygon tool, which is found under the Rectangle tool in the Toolbox, to bring up the Polygon Settings dialog (shown here). You can enter how many sides you'd like your polygon to have, and how "pointy" you want each side to be (using the Star Inset field).

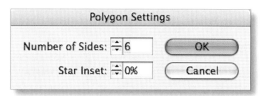

ADJUST POLYGON SIDES AND POINTS ON THE FLY

There's a little-known polygon shortcut that lets you adjust the number of sides to your polygon while you're creating it. While you're dragging (and you must be dragging—it doesn't work if you're stopped), just press the Up Arrow key on your keyboard to increase the number of sides, and the Down Arrow key to decrease them. You can also adjust how "pointy" your polygon is by pressing the Left and Right Arrow keys as you drag.

   ## EXPERIMENT WITH SIZE

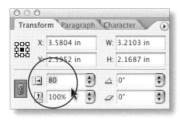

If you're resizing an object and you're not sure of the exact percentage you want to scale up (or down, for that matter), here's a tip that can save you some time. Once you've entered your percentage in either the Control or Transform palette, don't just press Enter. Instead, press Shift-Enter. That way, it applies the scaling, but if it's not the right amount (and if you're guessing, your first guess probably isn't) the scaling field remains highlighted; so you can simply type in another guess without having to re-highlight the field manually. Yeah, it's a small thing, but things like this add up fast.

THE SUBTLE ART OF FRAME SCALING

Here's a really helpful tidbit that can save you lots of time and aggravation. If you've created a frame and imported a graphic into it, and then you want to scale the frame, the tool you use makes all the difference. What I mean by this is if you click on a frame with the Selection tool (the black arrow), when you scale the frame (by pressing Shift-Command [PC: Shift-Control] and dragging), it scales both the frame and the object inside it at the same time. However, if you switch to the Direct Selection tool (the hollow arrow) and click in the frame, it scales only the graphic inside the frame and not the frame itself. (Although it looks as if the frame is scaling along with it, when you switch back to the Selection tool and click on the frame, you'll see that the frame is still the same size, but the graphic inside has been scaled up.) See, it's the little things.

 DON'T COPY AND PASTE IT—DUPE IT

If you want a duplicate of an object or text block, don't waste time copying and pasting (it's way too slow). Instead, just Option-click (PC: Alt-click) on the object with either the Selection or Direct Selection tool and drag yourself off a duplicate (it's called "drag copying"). When you hold the Option (Alt) key and click, your cursor changes into a double-arrow (as shown here) to let you know you're about to "drag copy." When you do this, you just see a copy of the duplicated frame (as shown) until you release the mouse button, and then you'll see the frame's contents.

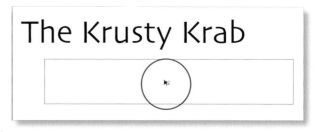

The Krusty Krab

SELECT AN OBJECT BEHIND ANOTHER OBJECT

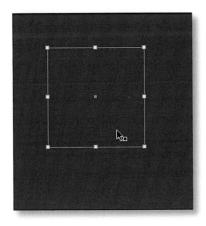

If you want to move an object (some text, a graphic, whatever) but that object is covered by another object, just Command-click (PC: Control-click) on the covering object and the object directly behind it will become selected (as shown in the example). If the top object is covering more than one object (in other words, there are objects layers-deep behind it), keep Command-clicking (each click selects the next object back) until the object you want becomes selected. (Here we've selected a square behind a dark blue object.)

   SELECT AN OBJECT BEHIND ANOTHER (VERSION 2)

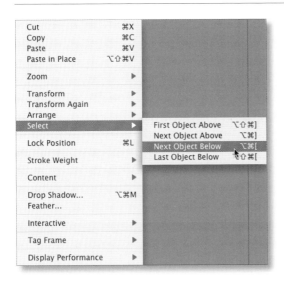

Another quick way to select an object that is behind another object is to Control-click (PC: Right-click) on the top object and from the pop-up menu that appears, go under Select and choose Next Object Below (as shown here).

SEND OBJECTS FORWARD OR BACKWARD

If one object is covering another object, you can send the top one behind the covered one by clicking on the top object and pressing Command-[(PC: Control-[). This sends the top object backward. In the example shown here, the star was covered by a large blue square, but we clicked on the square and used the shortcut to send that object back behind the star, making it visible (as shown). If at this point you want the blue box to cover the star again, just click on the box, then press Command-] (PC: Control-]) to bring it forward.

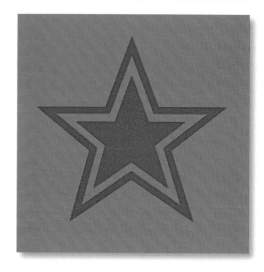

   KEEP ON SENDING OBJECTS FORWARD AND BACKWARD

Another way to move objects in front of or behind other objects is to select the top object, then Control-click (PC: Right-click) and in the pop-up menu that appears, go under Arrange and choose Send Backward to move the current object back one level, or choose Send to Back to move the object as far back as it can go on that layer (meaning no other objects are behind it).

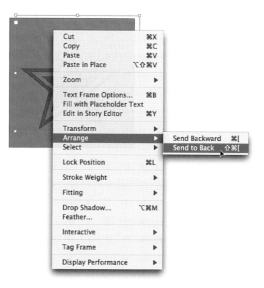

SET YOUR DEFAULT FILL AND STROKE COLORS

InDesign's default fill and stroke settings are no fill with a black stroke, but you can change that to anything you'd like. Just launch InDesign but don't open any documents. While no documents are open, go to the Swatches palette, click on the Fill icon and choose your new default fill color, then do the same for the stroke. These are now your default settings.

   ## AUTO ADD/DELETE PATH POINTS

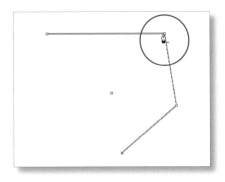

If you're drawing a path with the Pen tool and you decide you want to delete a point you've created, you go back to the Toolbox and choose the Delete Anchor Point tool, right? You don't have to. You can add and delete points using the regular Pen tool; and best of all, you don't even have to memorize a shortcut—just move your Pen tool over an existing point and it immediately changes to the Delete Anchor Point tool (as shown here)—so you can just click on that point and it's gone. Want to add a point? Just move your Pen tool directly over an existing path and it immediately turns into the Add Anchor Point tool, so you can just click to add a point. Move away from the path, and you're back to the regular ol' Pen tool.

MOVE JUST ONE SIDE OF YOUR CURVE

If you've created a curve using the Pen tool, when you go to adjust that curve you'll see two direction lines. They kind of work like a teeter-totter in that when you adjust the direction point on one side of the line, the other side of the line moves in reaction (one side goes up, the other side goes down). But there's a little-known trick that lets you adjust just one side of the direction lines, leaving the other side undisturbed. Just 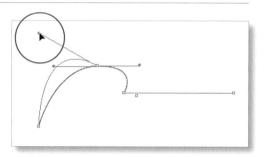 press Shift-C to switch to the Convert Direction Point tool, then use it to click on one direction point on one of the direction lines (as shown here). Now when you make your adjustment, it affects only that one side. This, my friends, will change your life (well, at least your life as it relates to editing paths).

   HOW TO STOP ONE PATH AND START ANOTHER

If you're drawing an open path, and want to stop drawing that path and move on to another (without actually closing the old path), try this: Move your cursor to an area away from your original path and Command-click (PC: Control-click). This deselects the first path, and now you're ready to move on to your next path.

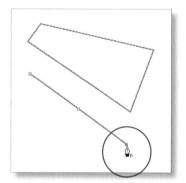

   HOW TO REMOVE ONE DIRECTION POINT FROM A CURVE

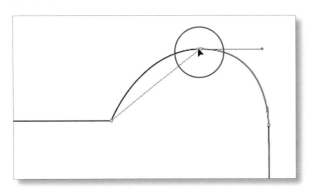

Ya know how curve anchor points have two direction lines and two direction points? Well, they don't have to—if you prefer that just one side of the curve is curved and the other side is straight, you can delete the other side of the curve. Here's the trick: Use the Direct Selection tool to select the anchor point of the curve that has the direction line you want to delete, then drag the direction point back in toward the center until it actually touches the curve's anchor point. You're basically just tucking it back in. When it hits that anchor point—it's gone—that side of the curve now becomes a straight segment (as shown here).

   CUTTING THE CHEESE (OR MAKING A PERFECT HALF CIRCLE)

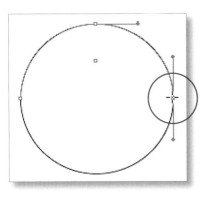

If you've ever tried to draw a half circle, you know how frustrating it can be. This tip will make you look like an expert with the Pen tool (even though you won't be using the Pen tool at all). Use the Ellipse tool to draw a perfect circle (hold down the Shift key to constrain it as you're drawing it). Then use the Scissors tool to click (cut) the two side points. You can simply delete the half that you don't need, and you will end up with a perfect half circle.

   POINT IT OUT

When simple lines aren't enough to make your point, draw an arrow instead. Well, you can't actually draw an arrow; okay, you *could*, but who wants to? Draw a line and then go to the Stroke palette and make sure that you have chosen Show Options in the Stroke palette's flyout menu. Using either the Start or End pop-up menu, choose the arrowhead or tail that you like best. Make sure that your stroke Weight is high enough to show the stroke and arrowhead that you desire.

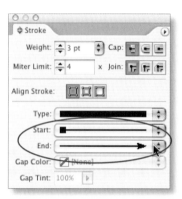

Turn The Page

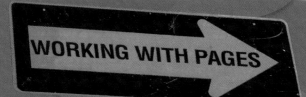

WORKING WITH PAGES

This is a big chapter. And by big I mean large. Do you see where I'm going with this? Because honestly, I have no idea whatsoever. Well, I have some idea, but I'm still

Turn the Page
working with pages

forming it as I go. In the meantime, this chapter is all about working with page layout, adding pages, changing pages, numbering pages, mastering pages, and even mastering master pages (and I'm not even sure that's a real thing). Now, what if you only work with single-page documents and therefore you never really "Turn the Page"? You still have to read this chapter. Why? Because at the end of this chapter we have a drawing for some fabulous prizes (selected especially for you), so make sure you put your business card in the box at the door when you're finished so you're entered in the drawing. (By the way, if you asked yourself anything along the lines of "Where's the door?" or "Did I remember to bring my business cards?" perhaps working with pages isn't your biggest concern.)

DRAG PAGES FROM ONE DOC TO ANOTHER

This feature of InDesign is very, very slick. If you want to copy a page from one document to another, you can literally drag-and-drop it. Here's how: Start by making sure both documents are open onscreen, then go to the Pages palette, click on the page you want to copy, and then drag-and-drop it right into the new page area (you know—the area within the margins) and the page will be copied into that document. That is mighty cool!

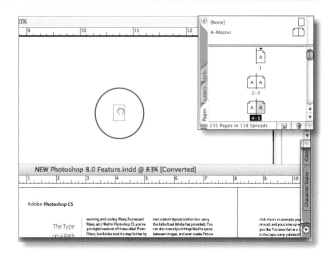

   WHEN ONE MASTER PAGE JUST DOESN'T CUT IT

Yeah, I know what you're thinking, you could just create two master pages, but hierarchical master pages kick multiple master pages' butt! Let's say that you're doing pages for a catalog and all of the pages will have your logo, website URL, and a color bar. However, the catalog will also be divided into sections and each section will have the section name on the color bar as well as other things that pertain to only that section. This tip will make that chore child's play. Create your first master page using the default A-Master Page that will be used throughout the document. Then, create your master page for the first

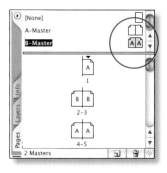

section by choosing New Master from the Pages palette's flyout menu. Now drag the first master page you created on top of the section master page, and your section master page will have all the elements on it from both master pages. When you make changes to the main master page, those changes will ripple through all your sections, too.

BE FLEXIBLE WITH THE SIZE OF YOUR LAYOUT

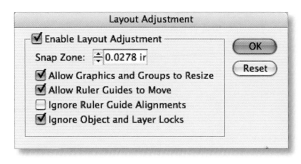

Change is inevitable and nothing is more frustrating than having to change your layout's dimensions. Say that suddenly the layout needs to change from tall to wide. Yikes! Rather than struggling to reposition all your elements manually, try this tip next time you need to make severe page size or orientation changes: Choose Layout Adjustment from the Layout menu and check the box labeled Enable Layout Adjustment. Now when you change your page orientation or dimensions, InDesign will do its best to keep everything positioned the way it was, but moving and resizing things to fit on the new layout.

   SPREAD BEYOND TWO PAGES

The next time you need to create a gate fold, try this tip: Open the Pages palette and turn off Allow Pages to Shuffle in the palette's flyout menu. Now when you drag pages next to each other in the Pages palette (you have to drag a page almost on top of the existing page until you see a black vertical bar, as shown in center), they will stay next to each other. Gate folds are typically three side-by-side panels. This tip lets you achieve that look.

 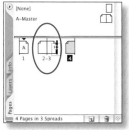 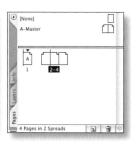

MAKE IT A TEMPLATE

If you're creating a document that is published repeatedly, you might want to consider making templates of your documents rather than opening them and performing a Save As each time. Templates are more efficient and less likely to corrupt on you as time goes by. As you open and save the same document again and again, you could have a problem that continues to build every time the document is used. With a template, you start fresh each time. Make all the frames and elements in your document that will be used each time it's published. Then choose Save As from the File menu. Change the Format pop-up menu to InDesign CS2 Template and click Save. The next time you need to work on the publication, just open the file through the File menu and it will open "untitled" and fresh.

   UNDERESTIMATING THE PAGE COUNT

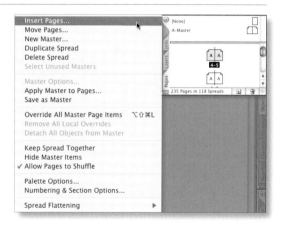

Okay, you need to add more pages. You've searched frantically under the menus and don't see a way to do it. For some reason, Adobe doesn't think that adding pages should be a menu command. Go to the Pages palette and either click the Create New Page icon at the bottom of the palette or use the Pages palette's flyout menu and choose Insert Pages to add more than one at a time.

ADD PAGES THE FAST WAY

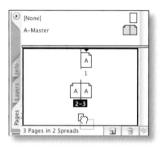

Do you want an even faster way to add pages to your document without choosing Insert Pages from the Pages palette's flyout menu and then adding pages manually in the dialog as mentioned in the previous tip? Instead, just click-and-drag the page icon from the top section of the Pages palette to the main section. Each time you do, it adds a page.

   LARGER PAGE ICONS

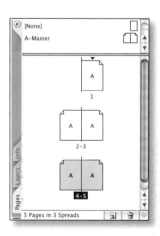

Admittedly, those page icons in the Pages palette are pretty small, but they don't have to be. If you'd prefer larger page icons, just choose Palette Options from the Pages palette's flyout menu, and a dialog will appear where you can choose your page icon size from a pop-up menu. (In the example shown here, we chose Extra Large.)

HAVE IT YOUR WAY

I guess people get really passionate about the way the Pages palette looks. I for one couldn't care less as long as the features are there. However, if it bugs you that the pages are listed vertically instead of horizontally, choose the Palette Options from the Pages palette's flyout menu and go nuts. You can even decide who's on top, Masters or Pages. Go figure!

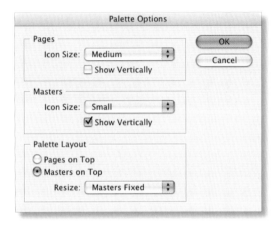

MAKE YOUR GUIDE STRETCH ACROSS SPREADS

When you're working with two-page spreads, if you pull down a horizontal guide from the top ruler, the guide only appears on the current page, not across the spread. If you'd like to have your guide appear across the whole spread (great for lining up blocks of text on facing pages), just hold the Command key (PC: Control key) before you click on your ruler, then drag it down.

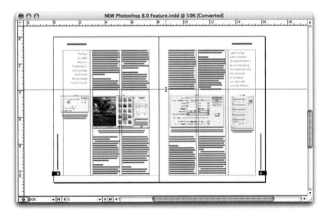

GET RID OF UNWANTED GUIDES FAST

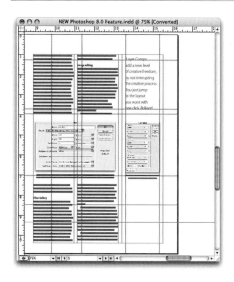

Want to get rid of some ruler guides fast? Just take the Selection tool, click-and-drag a selection over the ones you want to delete to select them (by default, when they're selected they turn the same color as the layer they are on in the Layers palette), then press Delete (PC: Backspace) to delete them. Tip: It's easier if you select guides either right above the page or to the right of the page in the pasteboard area, so you don't accidentally select other objects on the page.

 DELETE ALL YOUR GUIDES AT ONCE

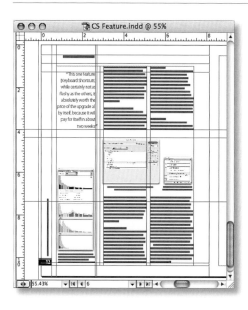

Want all your guides on a page or spread to disappear for good with extreme prejudice? Just press Option-Command-G (PC: Alt-Control-G), which selects all your guides, then press Delete (PC: Backspace) to erase them all.

ADD A GUIDE EXACTLY WHERE YOU WANT IT

Know exactly where you want your guide? Then instead of dragging it out from the rulers, just double-click in either the top or side ruler where you want the guide to appear, and it will appear right there. Sweet!

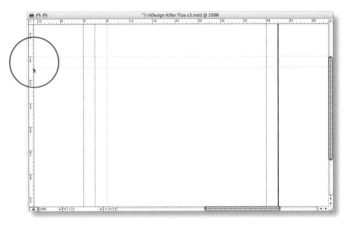

  GET BOTH A HORIZONTAL AND VERTICAL GUIDE

If you drag from the top ruler down, you get a horizontal guide. If you drag the left-side ruler, you get a vertical guide. But did you know that if you hold the Command key (PC: Control key) and click in the top left corner (where the two rulers meet) you can drag out both a horizontal and vertical guide at the same time?

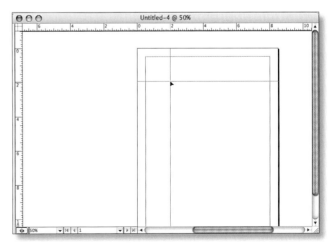

COPY THOSE GUIDES

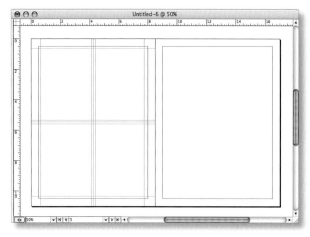

If you want to move the guides you have set up on one page to another page in your document (or in another document, for that matter), you can copy and paste them just like anything else. First get the Selection tool, then Shift-click on each guide you want to copy (to select them), then press Command-C (PC: Control-C) to copy them. Switch to the page where you want the guides and press Command-V (PC: Control-V). Couldn't be easier. If you're pasting these guides into a different document, make sure the document you're pasting into has the same physical dimensions or the guides will be out of place when pasted.

  ## SHORTCUT FOR LOCKING GUIDES

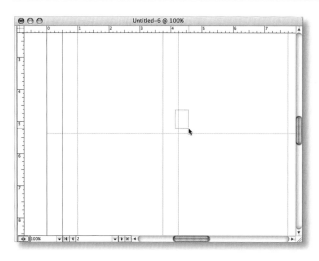

If you're using guides to set up your page layout, you usually don't want to move a guide accidentally, or it'll mess up your layout. That's why you'll want to know this shortcut: Option-Command-; (PC: Alt-Control-;) which locks all your guides down so they can't be moved. If you then try to select a guide (as we're trying to do in the capture shown here), it ignores your attempts. If you decide later that you want to unlock them, just press the same shortcut.

TOGGLE GUIDES ON/OFF

Here's one of the most useful shortcuts in all of InDesign. When you want a clean, no-guides look on your page (and by clean I mean no ruler guides, no margin guides, no column guides—nothing but page, baby), press Command-; (PC: Control-;).

Guides visible

Guides hidden

CREATE YOUR OWN CUSTOM GUIDES LAYOUT

Dragging guides from the rulers is so 1980s. The next time you need to get guides on the page and have them perfectly spaced apart, try this: Choose Create Guides from the Layout menu. Now you have a dialog with a Preview option to specify how many rows and columns you want and how far they will be spaced apart from each other, known as the gutter.

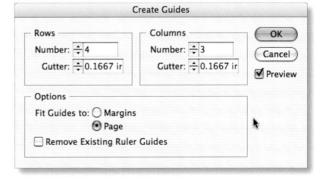

ASSIGN GUIDES TO A LAYER

Hiding guides (View>Hide Guides) is an all-or-nothing deal. Sometimes you only need to hide some of the guides but not all of them. This tip will make your life easier. In the Layers palette Option-click (PC: Alt-click) on the Create a New Layer icon and name the new layer "guides". Now use the Selection tool to select the guides you want on that layer. A little box will appear in the Layers palette at the right side of the layer that contains the selected guides. Drag-and-drop this little box to the new guides layer to assign them to their own layer. Now you can click on the Eye icon for this layer to turn it off or on whenever you want to hide or show the guides.

   GET ORGANIZED WITH LAYERS

Stop creating different documents to show different versions of the same brochure. Use layers instead. If most of your layout is going to contain the same elements but some of the elements and text will need to change, try putting the "changeable" items on different layers. You can create more layers than you'll probably need and it doesn't add any significant weight to the document, so go nuts. Bring up the Layers palette from the Window menu and click on the Create a New Layer icon to add layers (Option-click [PC: Alt-click] if you want to name it at the same time). Then select objects on the page. In the Layers palette you'll notice a tiny little square appears on the right-hand side of the layer that contains the selected object. Drag the little square to move those objects to their respective layers.

   SELECT EVERYTHING ON ONE LAYER

Select All does just what you would expect—it selects everything (except, of course, items on locked layers and master items). However, there are those times when you just want to select everything on a single layer. Here's a quick way to do it. Hold down the Option (PC: Alt) key and click on the name of a layer in the Layers palette. Now everything on that layer is selected, but everything else is left alone.

   STACK IT UP IN THE RIGHT ORDER

Stacking order is vitally important when it comes to printing with transparency. You should have your background images on the bottom, your photos next, then your vector graphics, and then your text on top. An easy way to accomplish this is to simply make layers for the aforementioned objects in the Layers palette. You can also reorder several groups of objects at any time by dragging a layer up or down in the Layers palette.

DELETE ANY LAYERS YOU'RE NOT USING

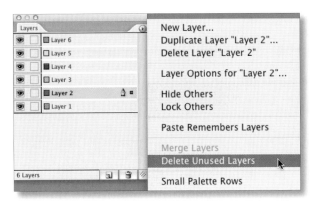

Got some layers you didn't wind up using (it happens pretty frequently)? Then choose Delete Unused Layers from the Layers palette's flyout menu and they're gone in a hurry!

   SEE THE REAL PAGE NUMBERS

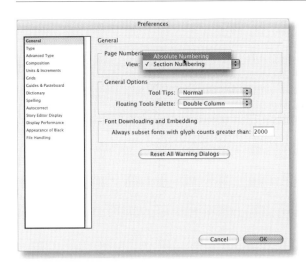

By default, the page numbers you see in the page number field in the bottom left-hand corner of your document window are based on the auto-page number-ing setting for your document. For example, if you created your document starting with page 326, the second page in your document will be page 327. However, if you want to see the real number of pages in your document, rather than the auto-numbering version, go to InDesign's Preferences (Com-mand-K [PC: Control-K]), select General, and change the Page Numbering View pop-up menu from its default setting of Section Numbering to Absolute Numbering (as shown).

   CREATE NEW SECTIONS (WITH THEIR OWN PAGE NUMBERS)

You can create a new section in your document, with its own separate page numbering scheme, by going to the Pages palette's flyout menu and choosing Numbering & Section Options. When the dialog appears, click the Start Section checkbox, then click the Start Page Numbering At radio button and enter the starting page number you want for your new section. Click OK and the

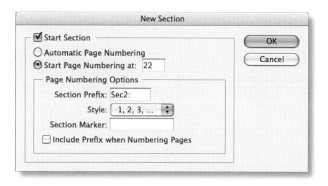

page you're currently on will start your new section. So within your document, you could have pages 1, 2, 3, 4, 5, 6, 7, then 22, 23, 24, etc.

   ONE IS THE LONELIEST NUMBER

Numbering pages automatically is child's play. But what about when you want page numbering to start on a specific page or to start over again on a specific chapter? Try this tip: In your multiple-page document go to page 3 and choose Numbering & Section Options from the Layout menu. With this dialog you can start the page numbering

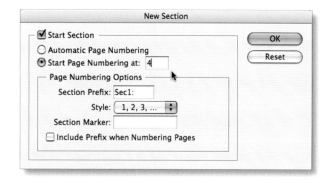

at a specific number, as well as change the style of numbering that will be used until the next section break or the end of the document.

JUMP TO THE PAGE YOU NEED

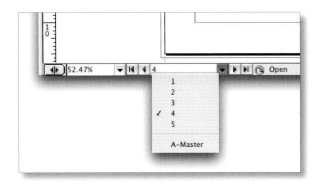

If you know which page you want to go to, there's a quick way to get right where you want to be—click on the down-facing arrow to the right of the current page number (down in the bottom left-hand corner of your image window).

   MAKE ALL MASTER PAGE ITEMS EDITABLE

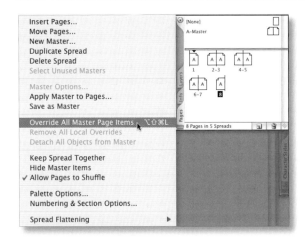

If you want to access all the items on your master page while you're working on a regular page, you're just one quick click away. Go to the Pages palette's flyout menu and choose Override All Master Page Items (as shown here). Now those master page items that were once "off limits" are live on your page (not just your current page—every page).

MAKE JUST ONE MASTER PAGE ITEM EDITABLE

If you want to edit just one master page item, just Shift-Command-click (PC: Shift-Control-click) on the item and it becomes live on your page so you can reposition it, move it, or even delete it. However, it only becomes live on your current page— it remains on the master page as far as any other pages in your document are concerned. If you truly want that item demoted from master page item to just a regular item on your page, once it's selected you can go to the Pages palette's flyout menu and choose Detach Selection From Master (as shown here).

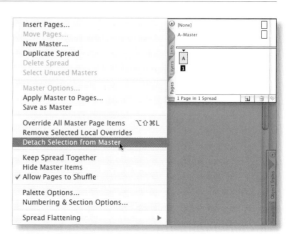

    ASSIGN MASTER PAGE ATTRIBUTES TO A PAGE

If you're working on a page in your document and decide you want the objects on a master page to appear on that page, just go to the Pages palette, click on the thumbnail for the master page you want to apply, and drag-and-drop it right onto the page thumbnail icon for the page you're on. This applies the master page attributes to that page.

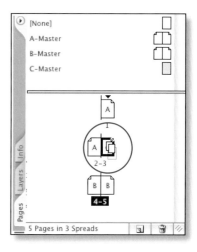

YOU WILL BE ASSIMILATED

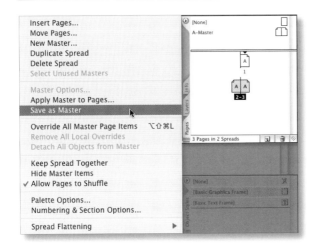

You've created such a wonderful page that you want all other pages in your document to look like it. However, you didn't create it on a master page. No problem, simply choose Save As Master from the Pages palette's flyout menu.

   ## FROM TEXT FRAME TO GRAPHICS FRAME FAST

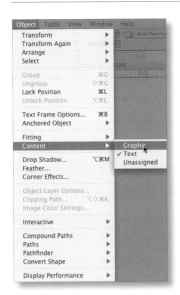

If you like to set up your pages with all the text and graphics frames before any actual content is added to the page, then you'll really find this helpful. If you have a text frame in place and decide you want to use it to hold a graphic instead, you don't have to delete the text frame and create a new graphics frame—just change its frame type by clicking on the frame, going under the Object menu, under Content, and choosing Graphic. The same works vice versa to change graphics frames into text frames.

MAKE A TOC STYLE

A table of contents sounds like a simple thing until you try to do one with InDesign. It doesn't have to be hard (it just is). A TOC Style is a set of options to build your table of contents. You can build a new one simply by choosing Table of Contents Styles from the Layout menu and clicking the New button in the dialog. Give your style a catchy name like "TOC Style 1." At this point all

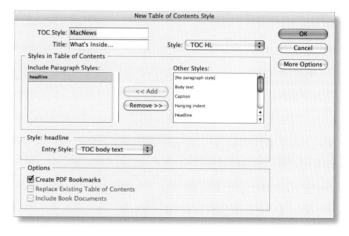

you really need to do is tell it which of your paragraph styles will be included as TOC entries and click OK. More tips follow.

   TOC: MORE OPTIONS

In the New Table of Contents Style dialog there is a More Options button. As usual this means, er, umm, more options are available. With more options showing you get the choice of where you want your page numbers, what kind of character (such as a Tab) is between the text entry and the number, and the ability to sort the entries in alphabetical order. See—I told you it meant more options.

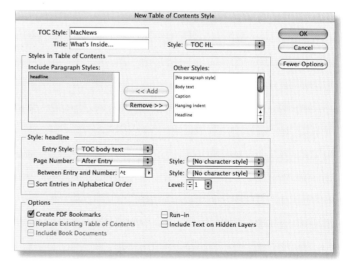

STYLE VS. ENTRY STYLE

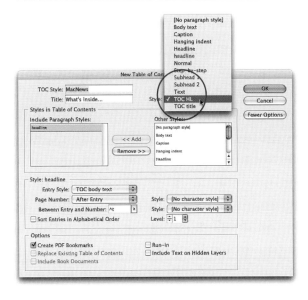

The New Table of Contents Style dialog makes too much use of the word "style." I mean it's all over the place. Let's face it, this dialog needs an overhaul. The easiest way to make sense of it is to remember that when you see just the word "style" by itself, it refers to stylizing the item to the left of it in the dialog. For example, if you wanted to pick a paragraph style for your title, you would choose it from the Style pop-up menu to the right of the Title field. Ahhhh, now it makes sense! Keep in mind that you should create all your paragraph styles first before trying to create a TOC Style.

   GIVE ME DOTS

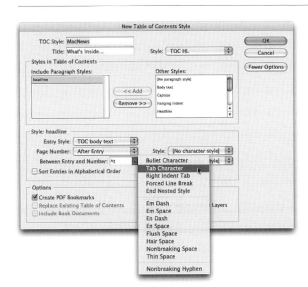

It's very common to have a series of leader dots between each table of contents entry and its page number. Click the More Options button in the New Table of Contents Style dialog and for the Between Entry and Number option choose Tab Character from the pop-up menu. Now to get the dots to appear you will have to create a Leader Tab in your Entry Style paragraph style sheet.

   LINK DOCS TOGETHER IN A BOOK

Just because InDesign can create a single document that's
9,999 pages long, that doesn't mean it's a good idea. If
you're working on a document that's going to be more
than a couple hundred pages long, it's probably a good
idea to think about breaking it up into smaller sections/
documents. You can still have the benefits of a single
document by using the Book feature. Create two or more
InDesign documents and then choose File>New>Book.
You will be prompted to save your Book document and

then you'll get a Book palette. From here you can use the Plus sign at the bottom of the palette
to add individual documents to the book.

   CREATE A PDF FROM YOUR BOOK

Once you have an InDesign Book
document, you can create a single PDF
from all the documents it includes. Simply
choose Export Book to PDF from the Book
palette's flyout menu. While you're in that
menu, check out the variety of cool things
you can do there. You know, like printing
the entire book. Hey, that could come
in handy.

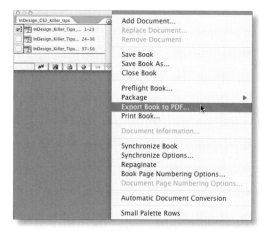

  ## SYNCHRONIZE A BOOK

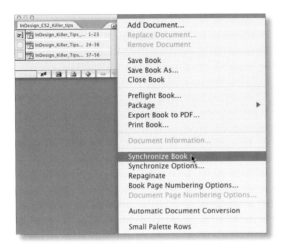

People are so helpful. They often want to take on some of your workload and ask nothing in return. Yeah, right! However, if you do have someone helping you create your book by supplying InDesign documents, you may want to make sure everyone's on the same page. Choose Synchronize Book from the Book palette's flyout menu to make sure that all the documents in the book have the same TOC, character and paragraph styles, as well as trap presets and swatches.

   ## BOOK PAGINATION

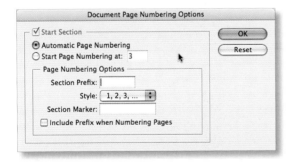

Page numbering is important, so use this tip to make sure that your book's page numbers come out the way you want. You can verify the page numbering options for each individual document in your book to make sure that they are all set to automatic numbering (or whatever you like) by choosing Document Page Numbering Options from the Book palette's flyout menu. Then all you have to do is enter page numbering options within the same menu to set your favorite way of numbering for the entire book.

CREATE INDEX ENTRIES

Before you can build an index, you have to specify some words that you want to appear in it. Unfortunately InDesign has no mind-reading feature so the program has no idea of what should be in the index and what shouldn't. Bring up the Index palette from the Type & Tables flyout menu under Window or hit Shift-F8 on the keyboard. Now simply highlight a word that you want included in the index and click the Create a New Index Entry button at the bottom of the Index palette. In the New Page Reference dialog you can choose the topic level and how the word is sorted. Once you hit OK, your word is added to the Index palette in alphabetical order.

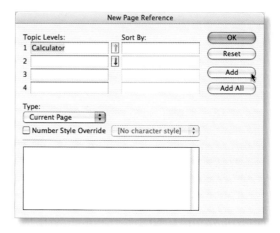

   INDEX CROSS-REFERENCING

Doesn't it drive you crazy when you take time to look up a word in the index of a book you're reading only to find "See blah blah blah"? Then you have to go look up another word. Well now you, too, can drive your readers crazy. When you create an index entry in the New Page Reference dialog, simply change the Type pop-up menu from Current Page to See, See Also, etc. Then in the Referenced field that appears under the Type pop-up, either type in the index entry that they really should go to or drag-and-drop the entry from the list of index items in the box below it.

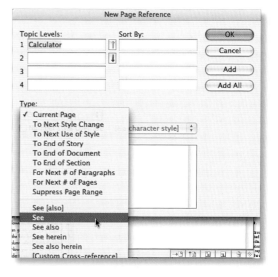

HEY, THERE'S NO PDF BUTTON ON THE BOOK PALETTE

True, but there is a Print button that you can use to create a PDF. Hold down the Option key (PC: Alt key) and click the Print button. Now you will be prompted to export to PDF instead of printing.

   ADD DOCUMENTS TO A BOOK FROM THE DESKTOP

Hey, we all enjoy navigating Open dialogs, but sometimes just to break up the monotony you can actually drag stuff from the desktop. Here's a tip for all you book lovers: With the Book palette open, simply drag an InDesign document into the palette from the desktop (or any other folder in your computer) to add it to the book.

I WANT JUST ONE DOCUMENT

Although the Book palette lets you treat multiple documents like a single big document, sometimes you just want to do something to an individual document. Maybe you only want to print one document in the book. Once you highlight a single document or multiple documents in the Book palette (Command-click [PC: Control-click] on all the documents you want to select), you can use the Book palette's flyout menu to choose your option. You'll notice that it now says it will apply commands to the selected documents; for example, Print Book becomes Print Selected Documents.

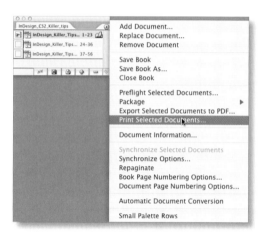

   ## TAKE IT TO THE WEB

With a book of multiple InDesign documents, going to the Web can be a challenge. I mean c'mon, who wants to open up and export individual documents? If you're doing that, stop it! Try this tip: Open your book document and from the Book palette's flyout menu go to Package and choose Book For GoLive. To take full advantage of this, you will need Adobe GoLive CS or higher. If you have GoLive CS or higher, you can then move the package folder into the

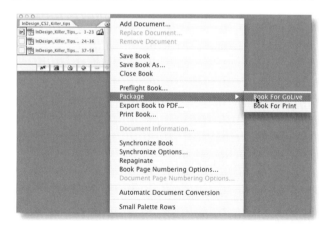

InDesign Packages area of your site and start to repurpose your content for the Web.

Contains Graphic Images

WORKING WITH GRAPHICS

Although there's a lot you can do right within InDesign, sometimes you have to reach outside InDesign and import a graphic. Yes, it's unseemly, but people (even fine

Contains Graphic Images

working with graphics

people like yourself) do it every day right out in broad daylight. If you're one of those (a graphic importer/exporter), at some point you're going to want some help, mostly some tips to make you faster, better, and all-around more gooder (gooder? I meant "bester"). Oh yes, that day's a-comin' and when it does, we'll be there. We'll be there to greet you with open arms and share with you a level of graphic tips so rich, so graphic, so graphically rich that one dare not speak its name. You'll be able to do things to imported graphics that would make a lesser man blush, a steady woman swoon, and small children pass out cold. You're about to become a "Graphic Master," and you'll command an army of tips so vast, and so powerful, that no QuarkXPress-using adversary would dare stand in your shadow. This is powerful stuff. Use it with great care.

CREATE A VIGNETTE WITHOUT LEAVING INDESIGN

Hard-edged photos went out in the 90s. The new craze is to have images with ragged or vignetted borders. If you want ragged borders, you'll still need Photoshop for that. However, you can create a nice soft-edge border with this tip: Select your photo with the Selection tool. Then choose Feather from the Object menu. Click the Feather and the Preview checkboxes and enter your desired feather amount or simply click into the Feather Width field and use the Up and Down Arrow keys to increase or decrease the amount of feathering visually.

   DON'T BE A SQUARE

Sure, we will all use the Rectangle Frame tool to lay out most things in our documents. However, with this tip you can add a little flair to your text and graphic frames. After you draw a frame, choose the Pen tool and click-and-drag it on the edge of your frame. You just added a curve point, which you can use to create a nice curve in your frame.

TRY OUT BLENDING MODES

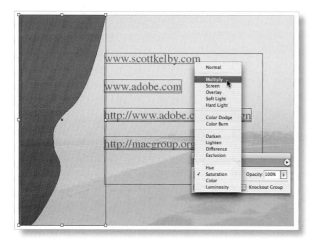

InDesign brings you the same blending modes you've grown to know and love in Photoshop. To create a nice effect without having to do it in another app, try selecting a vector shape filled with your favorite color (well, maybe one of the colors you're using in the job would be a better choice) that is stacked on top of another object and choose Multiply from the pop-up menu at the top of the Transparency palette. The beauty of this tip is that when you swap out the image underneath the vector shape, you'll get a different effect. Try the other blending modes and amaze your friends.

   USE THE PASTE INTO COMMAND

Putting a graphic inside of text always goes over well visually. The next time you have the text and graphic already on the page, try this tip to make use of what you already have: Highlight the text with the Type tool and choose Create Outlines from the Type menu. Switch to the Direct Selection tool, select your graphic, and hit Copy from the Edit menu. Then select your outlined text and choose Paste Into from the Edit menu. While you have the Direct Selection tool selected, you can still drag your image around inside the text to position it to your liking.

GOVERNMENT-MANDATED DROP SHADOWS

It's hard to pick up any publication that doesn't have at least one manually created drop shadow. Therefore, it's perfectly okay for you to have at least one if not several in your publication. You can create drop shadows on both text and images. Drop shadows and feathers are frame-based, so that means that even for text you select the frame with the Selection tool, not the Type tool. Once you have your frame selected, choose Drop Shadow from the Object menu. Click the Preview and the Drop Shadow checkboxes. Now you can choose the amount of offset, opacity, and blurriness.

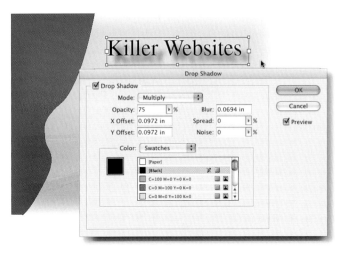

   CREATE FAKE GLOWS

InDesign really has no glow feature, but you can fake one using the drop shadow feature. Select your frame with the Selection tool (it works really nicely on large text) and choose Drop Shadow from the Object menu. Click on the Preview and Drop Shadow checkboxes, create a drop shadow with a nice glow color such as green or yellow, and choose zero for both offsets. Your text will appear to have a glow around it.

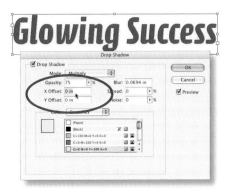

DRAG-AND-DROP FROM THE OS

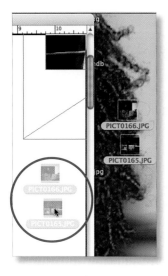

File>Place, File>Place, File>Place—that's what we do all day long to bring stuff into InDesign. There's a better way! It's called drag-and-drop. This tip will make your production go much faster. Chances are the graphics you want to place in your document are in a folder. Go to that folder in the Finder (Windows Explorer) and simply drag those images onto the page. You can even do more than one at a time. Just Command-click (PC: Control-click) on the graphics you want, then drag-and-drop them.

   ## SHOW IMPORT OPTIONS FOR MORE CONTROL

Get more choices when placing files by turning on the checkbox for Show Import Options in the Place dialog. With this option turned on, whether you're placing text, graphics, or PDF files there will be more choices of how those items are placed. For example, if you want to bypass the manual page breaks in a Word document, choose No Breaks in the Manual Page Breaks pop-up menu.

    PLACE PDF FILES TOO

InDesign can place PDF files on your pages. Big surprise, right? Of course, you'd expect that Adobe would allow you to place its own graphics standards, but the way you do it can determine how InDesign will import them. After choosing Place under the File menu, select a PDF. Then, from the Place PDF dialog, you can choose from

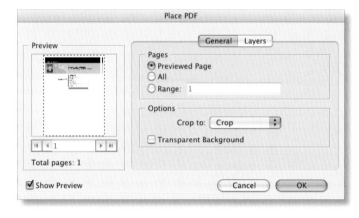

a number of options for placing your PDF. (Also, see "Import Multi-Page PDF" on page 250.)

    TEXT WRAP: TAKE IT OR LEAVE IT

Text wrap is a wonderful thing, but sometimes you want your text to wrap based on using different objects. Say you want to show your customer two different versions of a page and each version has a different main graphic but uses the same text. Here's a tip that will make your day. Put each graphic on its own layer and then

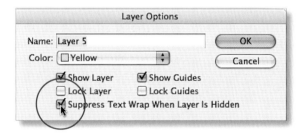

put the text on its own layer too. Then go to the Layers palette and double-click the name of one of the layers containing a graphic. In the Layer Options dialog, check the box labeled Suppress Text Wrap When Layer Is Hidden. Repeat this for each layer with a graphic. Now for each graphic, hide the other graphic layers and then in the Text Wrap palette (Window>Type & Tables>Text Wrap) set a text wrap to your liking. Now because you chose to suppress the text wrap in the Layer Options dialog, whenever you hide a layer it will also remove the text wrap for the graphic on that layer; when you make a layer visible, the text wrap will be there again.

WRAP IT, WRAP IT GOOD

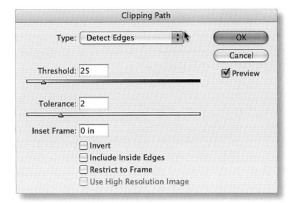

InDesign's text wrap makes text stay away from an object. However, with EPS and Illustrator files you can perform an extra step to get the text to wrap around the actual shape of the graphic and not just the frame. Select the graphic and choose Clipping Path from the Object menu. Then choose Detect Edges from the Type pop-up menu. Click OK. Now when you choose to Wrap Around Object Shape (the third icon from the left in the Text Wrap palette), your text will wrap around the shape of the actual graphic, not the frame.

   WHO'S THE MASTER NOW?

This one comes up a lot. Master pages are great in that they allow you to put something on a single page and have it appear on several pages in your document. However, there are those times when you need to do something to a graphic on a particular page but you can't because it's on a master page. But there's a way around that: Simply press Shift-Command (PC: Shift-Control) and click on the master page item you want to change on your page. Now you can do whatever you want to it because it's no longer tied to the master page.

FROM ONE VECTOR LOVER TO ANOTHER

Although Adobe InDesign and Illustrator are both vector-based, Illustrator's drawing tools kick InDesign's drawing tools' butt. This tip will give you the best of both worlds. Draw your cool illustration in Illustrator. Make sure you've set Illustrator's preferences (Illustrator>Preferences [PC: Edit>Preferences]) for File Handling & Clipboard to AICB (Adobe Illustrator Clipboard). Now copy your masterpiece, go to InDesign,

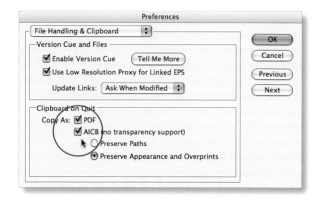

and paste it. If you use the Direct Selection tool, you'll be able to edit the points in InDesign that originated in Illustrator.

   I DON'T WANT TO DRAW NO STINKIN' BOXES

Designers just want to design. Working with grids and drawing boxes just seems so unnatural. If what you just read pushed your buttons, then you'll love this tip. You can place text or graphics into InDesign without drawing frames first. When you place a graphic or drag it in, InDesign will build a frame for it on the fly.

I HAVE TO DRAW BOXES FIRST. IT'S MY LIFE

If you're the kind of person who has to have structure in your world and the thought of placing a graphic with no predefined area for it to go into makes you nauseated, then by all means draw frames first. InDesign has about 11 million frame tools for drawing them. There are two main types: the ones with an "x" in them and the ones without an "x." InDesign actually doesn't care which ones you use. The "x"s are to make Quark"X"Press users feel better.

    MAKE THE GRAPHIC FIT

When a graphic needs to fit in a certain spot on your page, try this tip to make it easier. Draw a frame in the space you've allotted for the graphic. Now place the graphic in that frame. In most cases you will want the graphic to fit in the frame proportionally. With that in mind, choose Object>Fitting>Fit Content Proportionally.

SIZE DOES MATTER

Quickly, you need to resize a graphic. Whoa—when you grab the frame handle and pull, it just resizes the frame! This is the default behavior of InDesign. If you want to size the graphic and the frame at the same time, use the Selection tool and hold down the Command (PC: Control) and Shift keys as you drag one of the corner handles. This will resize the graphic proportionally.

 THE RESIZE-MULTIPLE-OBJECTS TRICK

Want to resize several objects at once? No sweat—just Shift-click on everything you want to scale (as shown here), then press Command-G (PC: Control-G) to group them together. Now when you grab a corner and drag outward, they all resize together. Note: This "group-it-then-resize-it" trick works on objects, but not on type.

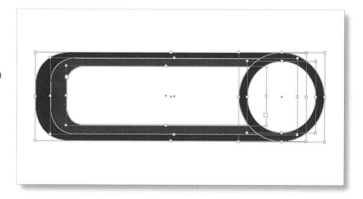

MOVE THE GRAPHIC WITHOUT MOVING THE FRAME

The frame is exactly where it needs to be. However, the graphic in the frame is not in the right position to show the part of it that you want. People often use frames to crop large photos, and you can "crop" a graphic by repositioning it in a frame so that only the part you want is visible. Use the Direct Selection tool to drag the graphic around in the frame without moving the frame. If you click-and-hold for a second, you'll get a live preview of the image as you reposition it in the frame.

THREE-IN-ONE

I want to move it, size it, and rotate it. Use this tip to do all three with one tool. It's called the Free Transform tool. That funky-looking tool in the Toolbox with the dotted box and the arrow icon can do three things. With the Free Transform tool you can move your graphics as well as size them (without holding down any keys) and rotate them. If you drag in the middle of the frame, you'll move it. If you grab a corner handle, you'll size it; and if you move just outside the corner handles, you'll be able to rotate it (shown here).

LOOK AT ME WHEN I'M TALKING TO YOU

Nothing is more distracting than to have the subject of your article facing away from the article or off the page. Don't go back to Photoshop; let InDesign flip your image. Use the flyout menu on the far right corner of the Control palette to Flip Horizontal.

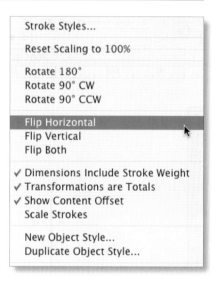

 DON'T USE THE FORCE TO ALIGN OBJECTS

Using the Force or your naked eye is probably not the best way to line things up on a page. The next time you need objects to line up, simply choose Align from the Window menu. Now select the objects that you wish to line up and then click one of the horizontal or vertical alignment icons on the Align palette.

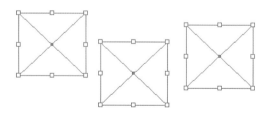

GIVE YOUR OBJECTS A RESTRAINING ORDER

If you want the objects on your page to be a certain distance from each other, try this tip: Using the Align palette, make sure that Show Options in the palette's flyout menu is on. Turn on the checkbox for Use Spacing, and type the exact spacing you want in the Use Spacing field. Select your objects and click either the Distribute Vertical or Distribute Horizontal Space icon in the Align palette.

Before using Distribute Spacing

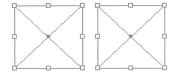

After using Distribute Spacing of 1˝

COPY AND PASTE IS SO 1980S

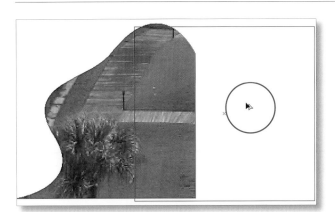

The next time you need to make a copy of something on the page, simply hold down the Option key (PC: Alt key) and drag the object with the Selection tool. This will make a copy of the object wherever you drag it.

STEP AND REPEAT INSTEAD OF COPY AND PASTE

Okay, I know there is some value to copy and paste. However, hitting paste 50 million times to get copies of the same object on the page is a drag. Try this tip: Select your object and choose Step and Repeat from the Edit menu. Now you can specify how many you want and how far apart they should be with the Horizontal and Vertical Offset options.

 DON'T MOVE IT TO THE SAME PLACE—COPY IT

Have you ever wanted to create a copy of something in the same exact place as the original? This is especially useful and necessary when you're trying to get things to be in the same place on different pages. Next time you need that, try this tip. Copy the object (Command-C [PC: Control-C]) that you want to appear in the same spot on a different page, navigate to that page, and choose Paste in Place from the Edit menu.

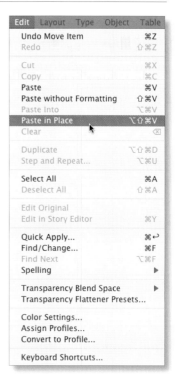

InDesign CS/CS2
KillerTips

PASTE REMEMBERS LAYERS

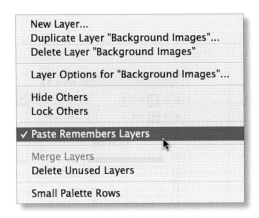

To keep things on the layers where they belong, you can use the Paste Remembers Layers option in the Layers palette's flyout menu. For example, if you have a photos layer and you want to copy a photo on page 1 and paste it on page 16, but you also want it to still be on the photos layer when you paste it, this tip makes it possible.

WHERE'S THE LIBRARY PALETTE?

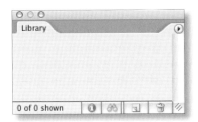

If you've looked for the Library palette under the Window menu (where all the other palettes are) you already know—it's not there. So where is this hidden palette? Believe it or not, you have to create it. That's right—you have to go under the File menu, under New, and choose Library. Then a Save dialog appears and you have to save your new library (and you can give it a custom name too). When you click OK, only then does the palette appear. Then, if you close the Library palette, to get back to it you have to go through the Open command in the File menu. If you think this is a weird way to access a palette, you're probably right.

  ADD OBJECTS TO THE LIBRARY

Now that you have your library created, rather than sit there and stare at an empty palette, you can either drag items from your pages into the Library palette or you can simply select an object and click the New Library Item icon at the bottom of the Library palette.

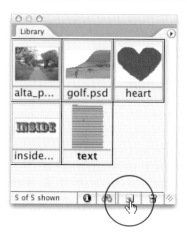

   DRAG FROM THE LIBRARY ONTO THE PAGE

Okay, you've got items into your library. How do you use them? Just drag them onto the page from the Library palette. You could also use the Place Item(s) command from the Library palette's flyout menu, but how much fun is that?

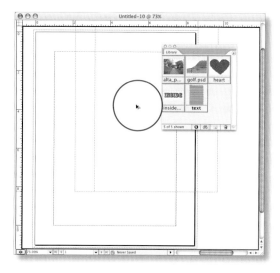

DOUBLE-CLICK LIBRARY ITEMS TO NAME THEM

If you created an object or frame and dragged it into a library, most likely it went into your library as "Untitled." That's going to make it hard to search for later. Use this tip to name your library items: Open your library and double-click each item you wish to name in the Library palette. When the Item Information dialog appears, simply key in a better name and click OK.

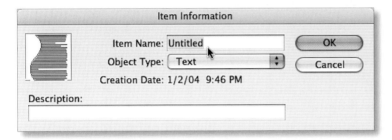

  SAVE TIME SEARCHING IN YOUR LIBRARY

If you're adding items to your InDesign Library palette, you can save yourself some time and assign keywords (for searching purposes) right when you add each object to your library. Just hold the Option key (PC: Alt key) before you drag the item into the Library palette, and the Item Information dialog will appear so you can assign your keywords in the Description field at the same time. Big time saver.

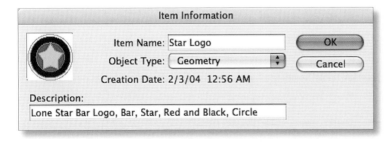

ADD KEYWORDS TO ITEMS ALREADY IN THE LIBRARY

If you want to add
keywords to items
that are already in
the library, simply
double-click on a
library item and
enter keywords
into the Description
field. Then you can
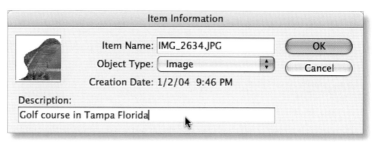
use these keywords to search for these library items later by clicking on the Show Library
Subset button at the bottom of the Library palette.

   SEARCH THE LIBRARY

If you have dozens
or even hundreds
of items in an
InDesign library,
scrolling up and
down the list look-
ing for what you
want will get old
pretty quick. The
next time you're
looking for some-
thing in particular,
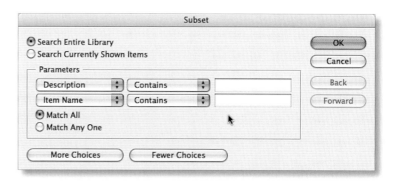
click the little set of binoculars on the bottom of the palette. This will bring up a Subset
dialog that allows you to search the item name as well as other attributes. Each time you
click the More Choices button you will be given the ability to add more choices to narrow
down your search.

NARROW YOUR LIBRARY SEARCH

Okay, picture this: You've done a library search using the word "logo" and about 60 logos show up in your search results. Not good. Here's how to narrow that search—once your search results have appeared, click the Show Library Subset button (it looks like a pair of binoculars) at the bottom of the Library palette. When the Subset dialog appears, click on Search Currently Shown Items, change the first Parameters pop-up menu to Description, then add another keyword. When you click OK, it will only search within the results of your previous search, helping you narrow things down to find the item you're looking for.

  HOW TO RECOVER FROM A LIBRARY SEARCH

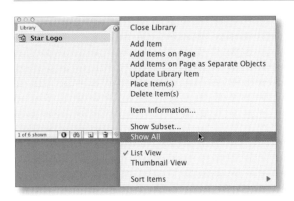

If you've done a successful search for a particular item, the library now displays only the item you searched for. Once you've used the item, how do you get to see the whole library again, and not just your search item? Go to the Library palette's flyout menu, choose Show All (as shown here) and all the items in your library will be visible once again.

  THUMBNAILS IN THE LIBRARY ARE COOL, BUT…

For a visual person, having thumbnails is cool, but they take up a lot of space. If you want to maximize your Library palette, try this: Choose List View from the Library palette's flyout menu. Now your Library palette will list all the names of the objects it contains and you'll see a lot more items in the same space than you did with Thumbnail View.

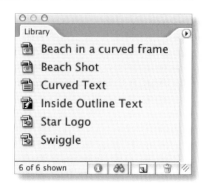

   DON'T PRINT THIS!

Hey, sometimes you just want something on the page for show. Maybe it's a note to your production department or some other logo or stamp of approval. With this tip you can make it non-printing. Select an object and bring up the Attributes palette from the Window menu. Now simply click the Nonprinting checkbox.

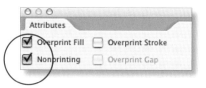

GO STAND IN THE CORNER AND THINK ABOUT WHAT YOU'VE DONE

 By default all operations in the Control palette affect selected objects from the center of the object. You can change that behavior with this tip: The icon on the left side of the Control palette has nine handles. You can click on any one of those handles to dictate where your measurements and operations will happen. We like the upper-left corner best, don't ask why.

   ## RELINK TO A NEW GRAPHIC

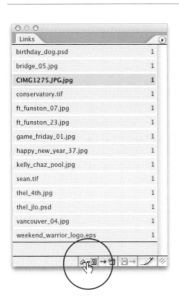 Your client gave you a picture and you placed it. But since then you've rotated it, you've scaled it, you've done all kinds of things to it to get it just the way you wanted it on the page. Now the phone rings and your client says, "Use the other picture"! Skip all those four-letter words, and try this: Bring up the Links palette from the Window menu and hit the Relink button at the bottom. Now select the other picture and click Open. Your picture will be replaced and all your transformations will be intact.

   REPLACE GRAPHICS

It happens. You've changed your mind and you want to use a different graphic. No problem. Select the graphic that you want to replace on the page and choose

Place from the File menu. Find your new graphic and make sure that at the bottom of the Place dialog you have Replace Selected Item checked. When you bring in the new graphic, it will automatically replace the selected one in the same frame.

   MAKE A PICTURE

Sometimes a PDF just won't do. You may need a graphic from your layout for your website or an image to send to a client. The next time you need a JPEG of an image on your page, try this tip: Select the objects you want to be in the JPEG file. Choose Export from the File menu, then select JPEG as the Format, and click Save. When the Export JPEG dialog appears choose Selection instead of Page. You can set the quality and then click the Export button.

WHO TOOK THAT PLACED DIGITAL PHOTO? INDESIGN KNOWS

If you place a digital photo into InDesign and you want to credit the photographer who took the shot, InDesign might be able to tell you. Click on the photo, then go under the File menu and choose File Info. This brings up a dialog that displays information embedded into the digital photo itself. In the left column, click on Description (as shown) and if the photographer who took the shot entered his copyright info, you'll see the author's name (as shown here). In the File Information dialog highlight the author/photographer's name and hit Command-C (PC: Control-C) on the keyboard. Hit Cancel to close the File Info window. All you have to do now is create a text frame under or at the side of your photo and paste in the photographer's name.

 FADE THAT IMAGE BACK

Sometimes you just want to fade or backscreen an image into the background. The next time you want that look, select your image with the Selection tool and drag the Opacity slider to the left in the Transparency palette.

  STACKING ORDER IS EVERYTHING

Some people freak out at the mere mention of transparency in a page layout program; but transparency used properly does work! Simply follow the stacking order rules to eliminate the most common transparency issues. You can use layers to make it easier or you can simply remember to always put on top the items you don't want affected by transparency. A good thing to have unaffected by transparency is type. If you have a transparent object on top of type, the type will most likely rasterize. So to prevent that from

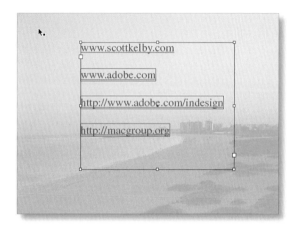

happening, put your background images on the bottom of the stacking order (or bottom layer), then your photos, then your vector graphics, then your body text and headlines.

   IDENTIFY PAGES WITH TRANSPARENT OBJECTS

Sometimes you don't want transparency, or maybe you want to make sure you're not using transparency on certain pages. This tip will show you which pages use transparency and which ones don't. Go to the Pages palette and you'll see that the pages with a checkerboard icon use transparency and the plain white ones do not.

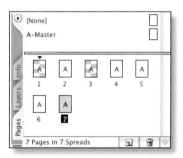

TRANSPARENCY FLATTENER STYLES

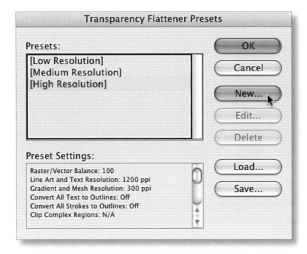

The key to successfully output-ting documents that contain transparency lies in the Trans-parency Flattener styles. Unless you're the printer or service provider, there is no way for you to know how to create a transparency flattener style that will work best. However, if you are printing your own InDesign documents with transparency, try this to improve your results: Choose Transparency Flattener Presets from the Edit menu. Three presets appear there by default. You can experiment with your own settings by highlight-ing one of the existing ones and clicking the New button. Adjust the sliders and options, name it, and click OK. You will be able to choose your transparency flattener style in the Print dialog's Advanced options. Experiment until you achieve your desired results on your output device.

USE TRANSPARENCY FROM PHOTOSHOP

Say goodbye to clipping paths. Photoshop has great tools for eliminating the background from an image. Well, now you can take advantage of that work in your page layout. Simply make an image transparent in Photoshop by putting it on its own layer and eliminating the Background layer. Save it as a native Photoshop file (.PSD) and then place (File>Place) that native file in InDesign. Once

it is placed, you can layer it on top of other elements and see through it.

   USE PHOTOSHOP ALPHA CHANNELS

Photo retouchers will often use alpha channels as masks or saved selections. The next time you want to eliminate the background of a placed Photoshop image, check to see if it has an alpha channel. Select the placed Photoshop image on your page and choose Clipping Path from the Object menu. Choose Alpha Channel from the Type menu. If there are alpha channels in the image, you will be able to choose them in the Alpha pop-up menu.

GENERATE CLIPPING PATHS AUTOMATICALLY

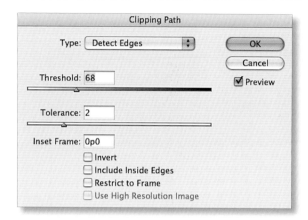

Although InDesign can bring in native Photoshop files with transparent layers, there are times that you will still have clipping paths. For example, older images that already have clipping paths in them or vector images that you wish to run text around. If you have an image with a fairly simple background that has not been erased in Photoshop, try this to eliminate it in InDesign: Place (File>Place) your image and then choose Clipping Path from the Object menu. Then choose Detect Edges from the Type pop-up menu. While Preview is checked, you can use the Threshold and Tolerance sliders to eliminate the background. Use the Invert option to eliminate darker tones. Click OK when you're done.

USE THE TRANSPARENCY FLATTENER PREVIEW

Printing transparency doesn't have to be hit-or-miss. The next time you're going to send your printer an InDesign document that contains transparency, you can use the Flattener Preview palette to see how your document will most likely look printed. Choose Window>Output> Flattener Preview. This feature is fairly processor-intensive, so it

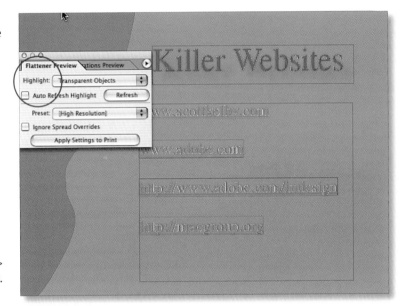

defaults to an off state. Choose from the various previews under the Highlight pop-up menu in the Flattener Preview palette to see which objects in your document contain transparency and more importantly which objects on your pages will be affected by transparency. You can also see what effect your transparency flattener styles will have on your document. Remember to set the Highlight pop-up back to None when you're done.

OVERRIDE FLATTENER SETTINGS SPREAD BY SPREAD

If you have a document that mixes both high-res and low-res graphics, then one transparency flattener style is probably not going to be enough. If your document contains mostly high-res images, then go to the spread that contains the low-res images and choose Custom from the Spread Flattening submenu from the Pages palette's flyout menu. This will bring up the same kind of flattener settings that you used in setting up your flattener style, but these settings will apply only to this spread.

Cool Hand Luke

WAY-COOL TIPS

As you might guess, there are a bunch of tips that are so cool they defy categorization. They don't belong in page layout or navigation. They'd be out of

Cool Hand Luke
a bunch of way-cool tips

place with those "nerdy" tips. These are the tips that you'll find hanging out with the cool kids. Sipping champagne with P. Diddy and rollin' in a Bentley bling-blingin' it with some 20-inch rims. These tips are so cool they can't be confined by convention. These are tips untrammelled. They need to bust out on their own, free to roam and spread their innate coolness wherever the pages take them. These are the tips you take out for a spin. The ones you use to impress your friends and humiliate your enemies. The ones you casually pull out at InDesign parties out in L.A. (Do they really have InDesign parties out in L.A.? Not without these tips they don't.) So use these sparingly. Pull them out when you need 'em—when you need to stake your claim, mark your territory, and generally establish who's the "king" of InDesign. Because remember, when you strip away all the typography, all the design, and all the CMYK separations, it all comes down to this—"Whoever dies with the most tips wins."

THE TRICK TO SHRINKING YOUR INDESIGN FILE SIZE

If you've ever taken a look at the file size of your InDesign documents, you've probably noticed that they get pretty big pretty quick, and that normally doesn't create a problem—unless you're emailing your pages (which we do quite often). Well, here's a neat trick for greatly shrinking the file size of a bloated InDesign document. Reopen the file in InDesign, then change something. Anything. Move a guide, type a space, etc., and then don't just choose Save: Instead go under the File menu, choose Save As, and save over the old file using the exact same name. For some reason, when you Save As (using the same name) it creates a much smaller file size for the exact same document. Sounds crazy, but it works like a charm.

 COPY DROP SHADOWS WITH THE EYEDROPPER

Putting a drop shadow on an image or text is easy (just select it with the Selection tool and go to Object>Drop Shadow). However, after you've tweaked that shadow to get it just right, you may need to apply the same shadow to another object or objects in the document. Drop shadows are a frame attribute and therefore you can use the Eyedropper tool to add the same shadow to other elements. Simply select the other objects by Shift-clicking on them with the Selection tool, switch to the Eyedropper tool, and then click on the edge of the frame containing the shadow. All your selected frames will have the same shadow settings with just a single click. It's tricky at times and works best if you click just to the right of the frame's edge.

  USE MULTIPLE VIEWS OF THE SAME DOCUMENT

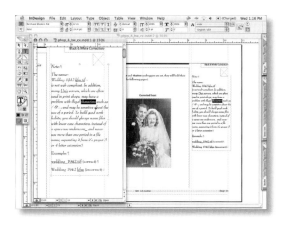

Sometimes you need to be zoomed in and out at the same time. Without causing a rift in the space-time continuum, you can simply choose Window>Arrange>New Window. This will give you another view of the same document that you can zoom in or out on. You can even tile the windows to see both views at the same time.

  WANT TO SPEED UP INDESIGN? TURN OFF PLUG-INS

For the most part, InDesign is an application made up of plug-ins. This allows Adobe and third parties to change and add to InDesign without the delays we often see in other products. InDesign also includes lots of functionality that you may not need. Therefore, you can speed things up by turning off plug-ins that you don't use. Choose Configure Plug-ins from the InDesign menu (PC: Edit menu), and then click Duplicate because you're not able to modify the default set. Then, turn off plug-ins that you don't use by clicking on the checkmark in the left-hand column next to each of them, such as the Hyperlinks Panel (as shown here), then click OK. You have to quit and relaunch InDesign for your changes to take effect.

IMAGE-BY-IMAGE HIGH-QUALITY DISPLAY

If you're wondering why your images sometimes look as if you're seeing them through a burlap sack, it's because InDesign defaults to a Typical Display view—typical of 1986 page-layout apps, that is. Well, you don't have to live with this anymore. Simply Control-click (PC: Right-click) on your image with the Selection tool. This will bring up the contextual menu and from there you can choose Display Performance>High Quality Display. This works on any kind of image in an InDesign document, but works extremely well on native Illustrator, EPS, and PDF files placed in your

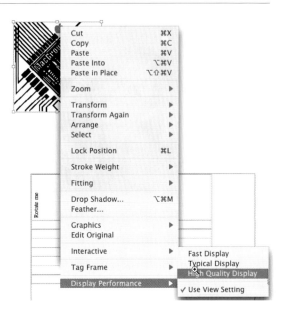

   SET YOUR OWN DISPLAY PERFORMANCE

As mentioned in the previous tip, you can control the display of your graphics on a frame-by-frame basis. But what's even cooler than that is that you can really fine-tune the difference between Optimized, Typical, and High Quality Display. Just go to the InDesign menu (PC: Edit menu), under Preferences, and choose Display Performance. Then, in the Adjust View Settings section, you can decide on the image quality for each setting.

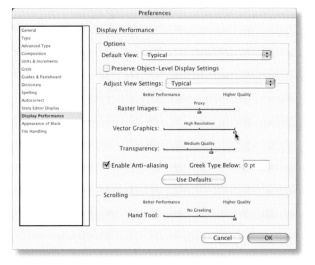

CREATE BLEEDS AND SLUGS WITHOUT OVERSIZED PAGES

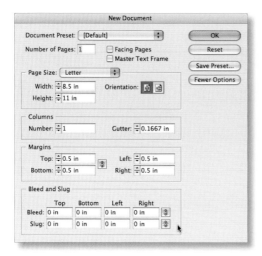

Hey, are you still creating oversized pages just to represent your bleed and slug information? Now you don't have to anymore. The New Document dialog allows you to create extra space around your document page for either bleed or slug information. Just click on the More Options button in the New Document dialog and you'll be presented with two extra sets of measurements at the bottom. You can enter measurements for either the bleed or the slug. This way, you can create your document at the actual finished size, yet still account for all the extra stuff that you have to put outside the document area. You can even control whether or not the bleed or the slug will print in the Marks and Bleed section of the Print dialog.

   VIEW BLEEDS AND SLUGS USING PREVIEW

Creating extra space around your document to represent the bleed or the slug is one thing, but what about viewing this information? Or better yet, turning this extra space off when you don't want to see it. In addition to the Normal View and Preview Modes, InDesign offers you Bleed Mode and Slug Mode. You can get to these extra views at the bottom of the Toolbox by simply holding down your mouse button on the Preview Mode icon and you'll get a choice among Preview, Bleed, and Slug.

   USE PATHFINDER TO JOIN SHAPES

Drawing irregular-shaped frames with the Pen or Polygon tool is okay, but sometimes it's a lot easier to just take two shapes and join them together. Simply draw two or more overlapping shapes with InDesign's various shape tools. Then, using the Selection tool, hold down the Shift key and select each shape. Now, choose Pathfinder from the Window menu. Once the Pathfinder palette appears, click the first icon to join them together as one frame for text or graphics.

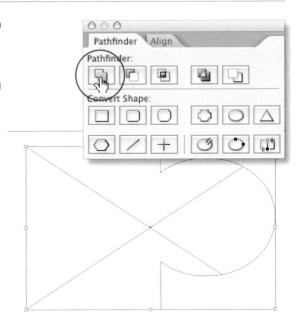

   ENTER MEASUREMENTS IN YOUR UNIT OF CHOICE

Everyone has his or her favorite unit of measurement. For many, it's inches. However, there are those times when you need to enter points, picas, etc. into a dialog. Well, without changing your Preferences, you can simply enter the measurement in your system of choice as long as you put the abbreviation for it after the numbers. For example, if you wanted to enter 400 points into a dialog that's expecting inches, you would simply type "400pt".

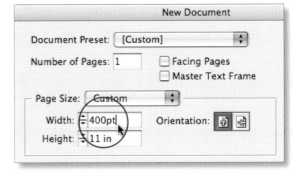

USE THE STORY EDITOR TO EDIT BLOCKS OF TEXT

Okay, there is one thing we miss from our old PageMaker days. Yup, you guessed it, the Story Editor. It's back, and the Story Editor is way-cool because it allows you to enter text and make changes or corrections to your InDesign documents in a nice, easy-to-read word processing-type view. Simply place your cursor anywhere in your text frame and choose Edit in Story Editor from the Edit menu. Now you can make all the changes you want, no matter how many pages your text spans or frames you have linked.

MacNews12–03.indd: Random Mac OS X Pant...

headline	Random Mac OS X Panther Tips
by line	by Terry White
Body	
Body 1st	It's that time of year again. The time of year that I try and pack as many useful tips in MacNews as I can. So in no particular order, here we go:
Body	
Subhead	**Drag Finder windows from any side now**
Body	Yup, this one was a pain before and used to be in OS 9. Now it's back. You can click on any edge of a window in the Finder and move it around.
Subhead	**Eject removable media from the sidebar**
Body	Mac OS X 10.3 (Panther) now has a sidebar on the left hand side that shows you your discs and most commonly used folders. If you have removable media such as a CD, Firewire drive or memory card mounted. You can unmount it by clicking the little eject button next to the icon representing your media.
Subhead	**Rename your flash media**
Body	I think that this was a bug in Jaguar, but it's fixed now in Panther. If you mount your compact flash (or other memory card) or even your camera via the USB cable, you can now actually rename the media card.
Subhead	**Color Labels are back**
Body	Click on a file or folder and from the new Action menu in a Finder window or the File Menu you can actually assign a color label to the file/folder you have selected. However, the hidden feature is that you can go to your View options and check the box for label so that you will get a column called Label in the finder window. Now you can click the Label column header to sort by Label.
Subhead	**Stuffit is cool, but Zip is built in**
Body	Mac users have compressed files for years using Stuffit. However, Stuffit is mostly a Mac thing. If you need to send files to users on Windows and you want to compress them. The best format is Zip. Now in Panther you can select your items and hold down the Control key and click your selection. When the contextual menu pops up, choose Create Archive. This will make a .zip file of your selected items and both Mac and Windows users will be able to decompress it.

OPEN QUARKXPRESS DOCUMENTS IN INDESIGN

Impress your friends! Open their QuarkXPress documents right in front of them inside of InDesign. InDesign supports opening XPress 3.3 through 4.1 documents natively. Simply go up to the File menu and choose Open. Point to your XPress document and click Open. Within moments the XPress document will be converted and opened as an untitled InDesign document complete with all its master pages, style sheets, and content.

    OPEN PAGEMAKER DOCUMENTS IN INDESIGN

Well, it wouldn't be fair if InDesign could open only QuarkXPress documents, now would it? InDesign can also open PageMaker 6.0–7.0 documents—with no additional plug-ins.

USE THE INFO PALETTE TO GET IMAGE DETAILS

It's 4:45 p.m. and the document you're working on needs to be in the printer's hands by 5:00 when you think, "Did I convert that image to CMYK or not?" With the Info palette, you can simply click on an image to find out not only what color space it uses but also what type of image it is and its resolution. If you don't see that information in the Info palette, just choose Show Options from its flyout menu.

  USE THE MEASURE TOOL INSTEAD OF RULERS

So—on your page is an image containing a person. You want to make sure your surrounding images are the same exact size as the person. One question remains. How big is the person? With the new Measure tool (found in the Eyedropper tool's flyout menu in the Toolbox) you can click on one side of the person and drag to the other side and the Info palette will show you exactly how big the person within the image is.

   UNEMBED EMBEDDED GRAPHICS TO MAKE YOUR PRINTER HAPPY

Embedded graphics are taboo with most printers and service providers. If you don't believe
that, call one and ask if you can embed all your
graphics in your next InDesign job and they'll
pass out right there on the spot. Luckily, if you
or someone else has embedded graphics in
a document you can select the graphic, go to
the Links palette (under the Window menu)
and choose Unembed File from the flyout
menu. InDesign even gives you the choice
of relinking to the original image or to a new
folder that it will create containing the unem-
bedded graphic(s).

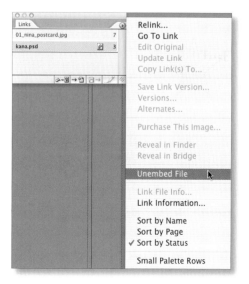

   YOU'RE THE ONE (LAYER)

Don't just click your way through your layers to turn
them off one by one in the Layers palette. By holding
down the Option key (PC: Alt key), you can click the
Eye icon of the one layer that you want to be visible
and turn off all other layers at the same time. This is
sometimes referred to as soloing.

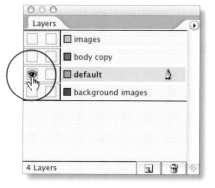

DRAG TO MAKE VISIBLE OR LOCK LAYERS

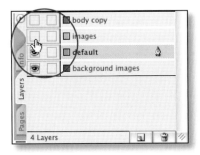

Although InDesign doesn't have any levers like the ones found in the Enterprise's transporter room, it has something just as cool: You can drag the visibility or locking/unlocking of layers. That's right, just click-and-drag through the column of Eye or Pencil icons in the Layers palette to make several layers visible/invisible or locked/unlocked all at once. You can even make the transporter sound effects while you do it. We won't tell.

Hidden Treasure

LITTLE-KNOWN
FEATURES

Are there really InDesign features you don't know about? Of course there are. If there weren't, how could we put together an entire chapter on hidden features? Here's the

Hidden Treasure
little-known features

thing: Every time a new version of InDesign is announced, Adobe boasts about the top 10 or so megafeatures that are sure to get lots of press. But each new version contains way more than just the 10 or 12 features you read about in the news. There are often nearly a hundred overall enhancements, improvements, and new features; but these are often overlooked due to space constraints or sheer lack of intestinal fortitude. So what happens to these "other" features? They remain hidden. Buried, if you will, in a cacophony of echoing nothingness until someone rises up to lift the veil of secrecy and expose these hidden gems to the light of day. It's not us, but surely someday someone will write a chapter on it. We can only hope.

   VIEW MENUS IN ALPHABETICAL ORDER

How much time do we all spend looking through the menus for that one command that we know is there somewhere? You just saw it yesterday, but you're frantically dropping down through the menus trying to find it. You know what it's called, but you just don't see it. You begin to reach for the manual but then you say to yourself, "Nah, that would take even longer. I'll find it eventually. Anything is better than looking in the manual." Try this: Hold down the Shift-Option-Command keys (PC: Shift-Alt-Control) and click on any menu. BAM, it's now displayed in alphabetical order.

View	Window	Help
Actual Size		⌘1
Display Performance		▶
Entire Pasteboard		⌥⇧⌘0
✓ Fit Page in Window		⌘0
Fit Spread in Window		⌥⌘0
Grids & Guides		▶
Hide Frame Edges		⌘H
Hide Hyperlinks		
Hide Rulers		⌘R
Hide Text Threads		⌥⌘Y
Overprint Preview		⌥⇧⌘Y
Proof Colors		
Proof Setup		▶
Screen Mode		▶
Story Editor		▶
Structure		▶
Zoom In		⌘=
Zoom Out		⌘−

   WANT TO USE INCHES? TYPE (″)

A number of applications let you enter values in fields and then decide the unit of measure after you type in the value. (For example, if you want 72 points, you'd enter 72 pt, or for three inches you'd type 3 in.) InDesign also lets you type in the inch symbol (″) after the value. (For example, to enter 7.3 inches in a field, you'd just type 7.3″.)

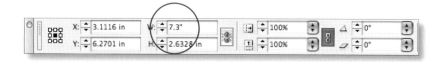

RESHAPE FRAMES WITH THE PENCIL TOOL

dimensions with units other t
percentage by clicking on the
and height fields.

t,

C. Assign a Resolution value (w

D. Select a color mode—I typ
if I ultimately want a CMYI
my RGB/Lab to CMYK con
devices.

is

ich

E. Be sure to turn on the Ant
all your graphic edges wil
transitions (a key to good-
based images). If you want
some reason, then uncheck

F. Click the OK button to compl

We get a kick out of this one every time we show it. The world is not just rectangles (unless you live in a Tetris game). You can modify the shape of your text and image frames by drawing on the edge of the frame with the Pencil tool. Just select the frame with the Selection tool, switch to the Pencil tool (N), and start drawing (make sure you start and finish right on the edge).

CREATE GRADIENTS THE EASY WAY

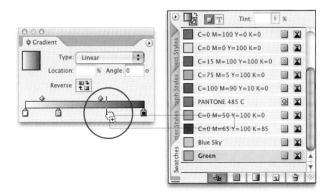

Creating gradients in InDesign used to be a lesson in patience. Now InDesign makes it much easier. Simply click-and-drag existing swatches from the Swatches palette to the gradient bar in the Gradient palette. Once you're done, you can even click on the gradient swatch in the Gradient palette and drag it back to the Swatches palette to keep your newly created gradient.

CHAPTER 8 • Little-Known Features   165

GET ROUNDED RECTANGLES WITH CORNER EFFECTS

Stop looking for the Rectangle with Rounded Corners tool. It doesn't exist. Create your rectangle frame with the regular Rectangle tool and then choose Corner Effects from the Object menu. From this dialog you can choose Rounded from the pop-up menu and then the amount of roundness you want in the Size field. Be sure to click the Preview checkbox so that you can see your changes as you make them. You can also use the Up and Down Arrow keys on your keyboard to adjust the Size up/down. Add the Shift key to change it by larger increments.

   ## RESET YOUR ZERO POINT

You probably already know that if you click-and-drag at the point where your rulers meet (in the very upper left-hand corner of your document window), you can pull out the zero point (the point where your ruler starts at zero). Many designers find this handy for measuring objects on their page; however, trying to drag the point back up into the corner is a little tricky. Luckily, you don't have to. Just double-click right up in that spot where the zero point used to be, and the zero point will snap right back into place.

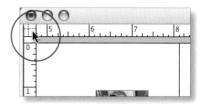

CHANGE ATTRIBUTES USING PERCENTAGES

Some people think in percentages. You know the ones. The folks who were in business school while you were in design school. They'll yell out things like "Make that 33% larger." When they do, don't reach for the calculator. This tip will make you glad that you slept through that math class. Simply highlight the text you want to change, and then in the Control palette highlight the field for the attribute that you want to change and key in the percentage. For example, enter 150% in the Font Size field to make your type grow by 50%. Now Tab out of it to apply it.

Before scaling 150%   **After scaling 150%**

  GETTING PAGEMAKER FEATURES IN INDESIGN

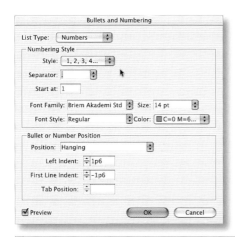

Since Adobe officially stopped developing or supporting PageMaker in early 2004, a lot of PageMaker users are making the jump to InDesign. If you're one of those, InDesign eases the transition a bit by making some of PageMaker's features and functionality available in InDesign (it kind of makes you feel a bit more at home). You can access PageMaker favorites like the PageMaker Toolbar, bullets and numbers, and PageMaker templates, plus training on how to make the jump to InDesign. For more details, visit Adobe.com.

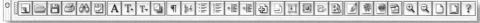

SEE YOUR PAGES BEFORE YOU OPEN THEM

Wouldn't it be great if you could get a preview of your InDesign document before you actually open it? It can't be done, but wouldn't it be great? (Just kidding.) You can do it, if you make one little change in InDesign's Preferences. Go into Preferences and choose File Handling. When the dialog appears, go to the Saving InDesign Files section and turn on the checkbox for Always Save Preview Images with Documents (as shown). From this point on, as you save or update documents in InDesign, you'll see a preview of those documents when you use the Open A File dialog.

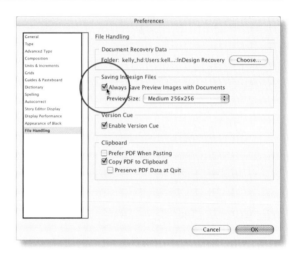

 THE DELETING STUNT

This is one of those tricks you'll only use when somebody else is looking (in particular, when a QuarkXPress user is watching you use InDesign). Just click on an object you want to delete within InDesign, and drag it right out of InDesign and straight into the Trash on your desktop (Mac OS) or the Recycle Bin (Windows) and the object will be deleted from the document. It's not a particularly practical tip, but it's great for showing off at Quark parties.

DRAG-AND-DROP FROM IPHOTO

If you're on the Mac, chances are you have a few photos in iPhoto. Wanna use those pictures in InDesign? Don't export, just drag-and-drop. That's right, simply create or open an InDesign document and launch iPhoto. Now simply select the image you want, and drag it right into your open document.

   ## DRAG-AND-DROP FROM ADOBE BRIDGE

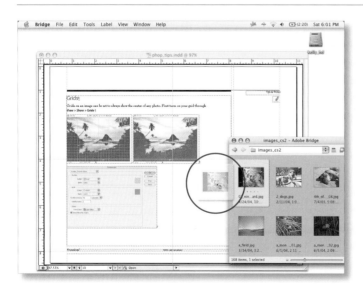

Adobe Bridge is awesome. It allows you to view hundreds of photos at once in any given folder. Wouldn't it be cool if you found that perfect photo and then wanted to use it in InDesign? Okay, do it! Open Adobe Bridge and find your image. Create or open an InDesign document and drag the image right into it from Adobe Bridge.

  CREATE A SPECIFIC-SIZED FRAME IN ONE CLICK

So you need a frame that's exactly 2.3x4.7″ and you've given up trying to draw it by hand? Stop pulling out guides. Simply choose one of the frame tools and click once on the page. Now you can specify whatever size you need in the resulting dialog and click OK.

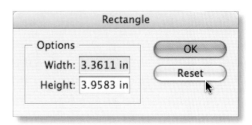

   CREATE A DUOTONE EFFECT RIGHT WITHIN INDESIGN

Okay, so you're on a budget and you can only print a two-color job. Well, there's no problem creating the text in any color, but what about your photos? Who wants to live with just grayscale? Colorizing TIFFs is not a new thing, but this tip will take it to a whole new level. When you select your grayscale TIFF or Photoshop placed image with the Selection tool and click-and-drag a swatch in the Swatches palette to the image, it will colorize the shadows. You've just faked a duotone without ever touching Photoshop. That's cool, but wait! Now simply click on a different swatch (don't click-and-drag, just click) and it will colorize the highlights.

ADD HYPERLINKS OR BOOKMARKS TO ANY OBJECT

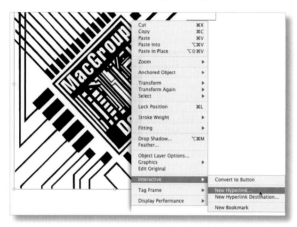

We sometimes wish that either print or the Web would go away; but guess what, they're both here to stay (at least for a while). This means that you'll sometimes create documents that need to get repurposed. We make PDFs all the time from InDesign documents, but here's a tip to make your PDFs just that much cooler. Select any image on the page with the Selection tool, bring up the contextual menu on it (Mac: Control-click [PC: Right-click]), and choose New Hyperlink from the Interactive submenu. You can now create a URL or Page link so that when the user clicks this image in the PDF, it will go to the webpage or document page of your choice.

LET THE GOOD TIMES SCROLL

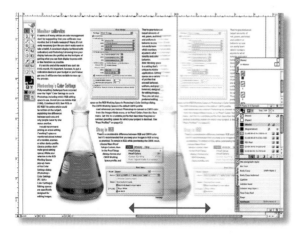

So you're one of those people who thinks a single-button mouse pretty much blows, and you've invested in a multi-button, optical mouse with a scroll wheel. You even took it up a notch and got a wireless one. Check this out—instead of just scrolling up and down your pages with the scroll wheel, hold down the Shift key and scroll left and right.

   SCALE SELECTED OBJECTS WITHOUT GROUPING

You've got 10 minutes before it's time to leave for the day. You just finished your layout, and your customer (art director, spouse… the list goes on and on) changes his mind and wants the layout to be printed on postcards instead of the original spec, which was a poster. Instead of reaching for the closest weapon, select all the objects (Mac: Command-A [PC: Control-A]) in the layout (yes, including the text), and go to the Control palette at the top of your screen. Make sure that your scale percentage fields are linked, enter a new percentage in either field, and everything gets scaled uniformly.

STROKE YOUR STYLES, BABY

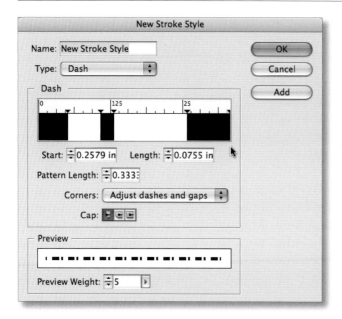

We all get very tired of the same old line styles: solid, thick-thick, thick-thin, etc. These line styles have been around for years, and using them shows the age of your design concepts. So let's break with tradition. You need a funky new line style for your funky new design (funky is a good word—or at least it was a few years ago). From the Window menu, get the Stroke palette and choose Stroke Styles in the flyout menu, and as quickly as you can, hit the New button so that you're not mesmerized by the existing styles. Now pick the kind of stroke you want in the Type pop-up menu and then design it by clicking in the area right below the ruler. You can drag the little triangles on the ruler to make the dashes thicker or thinner, or click on an empty white space to add another element to the line. To delete a dash, click-and-drag it down, and it will disappear. Once you've created a cool design, click OK.

   FOUR-COLOR PROCESS ON A SPOT COLOR BUDGET

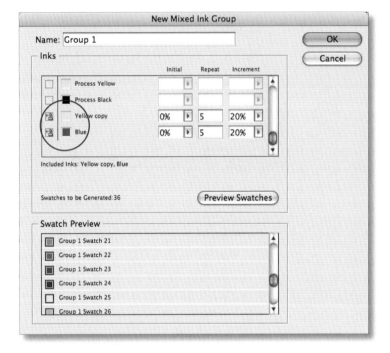

You want to create a kick-butt layout, but your customer can only afford two-color printing. Use this tip and save the day. Mix those inks! Create the two swatches representing your spot colors by going to the Swatches palette's flyout menu and choosing New Color Swatch. In the Color Type field select Spot, move the sliders to select your color, then click OK. You'll do this again for your second color. Now from the Swatches palette's flyout menu, choose New Mixed Ink Group. In this dialog you will see cyan, magenta, yellow, and black plus the two spot colors you created (shown circled in red). Click the little empty box in front of your spot swatches. At this point you have to do a little math. You have to give each ink an initial value (it can be zero), a repeat value for the number of steps you want, and then an incremental percentage for each step. Your goal is not to exceed 100% total. So whether you start out at zero and do five repeats at 20% each or 10 repeats at 10% each, you don't want to go over 100%. If you do, don't worry; InDesign will warn you and then cap it off at 100% anyway. After doing this for each swatch, just click the Preview Swatches button. This will show you dozens of swatches that you can use throughout your job, and no matter how many you use, you will only be using two inks at the end of the day.

COULD YOU PLEASE CHANGE THAT SPOT COLOR?

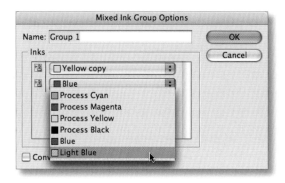

The phone rings. You check your caller ID and it's your customer with yet another last-minute change. This time, however, he wants to do the unthinkable. He wants you to change one of the spot colors you're using in your mixed ink group. I know, I know, it's bad enough that he wouldn't even spring for full color and here he is asking you to make a significant change like this. No need to think those thoughts. Go to the Swatches palette and double-click on the mixed ink group you created in the previous tip. Then in the Mixed Ink Group Options dialog, simply click on the pop-up menu with the swatch representing the color you want to change and choose the new swatch. BAM, all of your color swatches and the corresponding objects that you used them on will be updated! Don't forget, you still charge for the hours of work this would have normally caused you.

BACK TO THE FUTURE

Why is there screaming in the cubicle next to you? Did they lose power? Did their computer crash? No, actually they just hit Save when they meant to hit Save As. Now they've just wiped out a previous version of their document. You walk over and say, in your most sympathetic voice, "Let me see what I can do." Hit the Undo command (Mac: Command-Z [PC: Control-Z]) a few times to take the document back to the original and then choose Save As from the File menu. Yes, you just "saved" the day again.

   SOMETHING WRONG IN NEVERLAND? DELETE THE PREFERENCES

If for some reason InDesign is misbehaving and you want to start out with a fresh set of preferences, rather than hunting for them in your system, you can have InDesign automatically delete them for you. First, quit InDesign, hold down Shift-Control-Option-Command (PC: Shift-Control-Alt), and relaunch InDesign. A dialog will ask if you want to delete the InDesign preference files. Click Yes and it will automatically delete the prefs and create a fresh default set at the same time. (Note: If you're launching InDesign from the Dock in Mac OS X, make sure to click on the InDesign icon first to start launching it, and then hold down the keys immediately afterwards.)

   KICK THE KEYBOARD HABIT

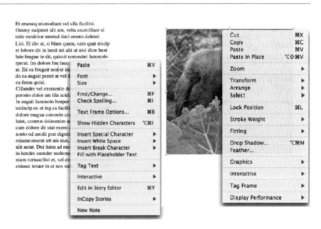

There must be a 12-step program out there somewhere for reducing your dependency on keyboard shortcuts. Actually, keyboard shortcuts are pretty cool, but I must admit that I know only a few. Therefore, I've become totally hooked on contextual menus. Try this tip the next time you're looking for a command to run on a particular object. Rather than wandering through the menus aimlessly, simply hold down the Control key (PC: Right-click) and click on the object to bring up a menu of the most commonly used commands for such an object.

GET TO THE UNITS/INCREMENTS PREFERENCES FAST

When you're working with type, some people prefer to work in points (usually typographers), some prefer pixels (Web designers), and others prefer centimeters (freaks). If you've got the Type tool and want to quickly get to the Units & Increments Preferences dialog to make a quick change or two, just Option-click (PC: Alt-click) on the Kerning icon in the Control palette and it will bring up the dialog for you—no more digging around in the InDesign (PC: Edit) menu.

  SPEED LANE TO THE MOVE DIALOG

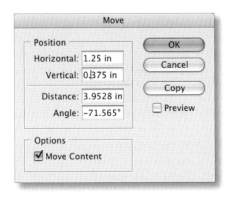

If you want to move an object precisely using the Move dialog, here's a quick way to get at it. Click on the object you want to move, then go up to the Control palette and Option-click (PC: Alt-click) on either the X or Y coordinate icon and the Move dialog (shown here) will appear. How's that for fast?

   SPEEDY SCALER

Okay, now that you know how to bring up the Move dialog, surely you'll want a quick way to bring up the Scale dialog, for resizing objects with extreme precision. Just click on the object you want to scale, then Option-click (PC: Alt-click) on either of the Horizontal or Vertical Scale icons up in the Control palette (shown here circled in red) and the Scale dialog will appear.

Portable People

MAKING PDFs

I don't get it. Why is this chapter named "Portable People"? See, this is what happens when people start using acronyms for everyday items—they lose touch

Portable People
making PDFs

with the meanings behind the acronyms. The "portable" part is the first word in PDF (which stands for Portable Document Format) and the song "Portable People" is from the band Ten Years After. (Sadly, I couldn't find a song or movie with PDF in the title, except for "Strawberry PDF 23" from the Brothers Johnson.) But do people care about that—about preserving the meaning behind the acronym? No. People are just too busy to pronounce full words anymore, so everything has to be an acronym. So basically, this chapter is about using IDCS2 to create PDFs so you can FTP them to a URL using DSL to UPS for NMR (that last one is the real acronym for Nuclear Magnetic Resonance. I threw it in just for effect).

PLACE A MOVIE IN YOUR DOCUMENT

Print and QuickTime usually have nothing to do with each other. After all, print is usually CMYK and static; and QuickTime is usually RGB and moving. So why would you ever want to place a QuickTime movie in an InDesign document? To go out to PDF and the Web. Choose Place from the File menu and then point to a QuickTime movie. You will be able to bring it in, and on your print document it will be a static image; but when you Export to PDF or Package for GoLive it will go out as a fully functional QuickTime movie.

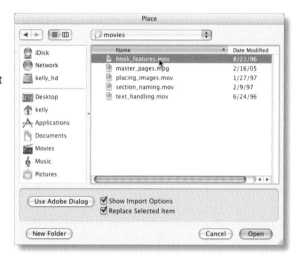

   PICK A DIFFERENT POSTER FRAME

Most QuickTime movies fade in from black. A black rectangle in your print document is probably not what you're looking for. So to avoid having a dull-looking print document, PDF, or website, simply choose an image as the Poster Frame (the frame that displays when the movie isn't playing). Double-click your placed QuickTime movie and in the Movie Options dialog change the Poster pop-up menu to Choose Image as Poster. Click the Browse button and go find a nice CMYK Photoshop image or TIFF to be used as your poster. You probably want to create the image ahead of time in Photoshop to be the same size as your movie so it fits seamlessly.

IMPORT A SOUND WHEN YOU DON'T HAVE VIDEO

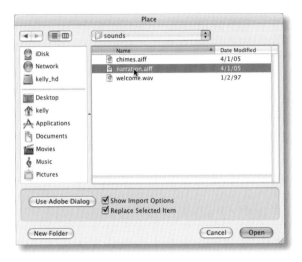

Placing movies is cool, but you can also place sounds. Why? Let's say you actually wanted to narrate your document to your client. You can record the narration in your favorite sound recording app, save it as a QuickTime movie and then place it in your InDesign document. Now when you export it to PDF the sound will go with it. You might want to check out other tips in this chapter to create multimedia buttons that will play your sound.

 FLASH IN THE PANTS

Another tip to spruce up your InDesign-generated PDFs would be to add Flash (.SWF) animation. You can place .SWF files just like you do movies. However, once you place your .SWF animation you will need to double-click on it, and in the Movie Options dialog enable the Play on Page Turn option to get it to start playing/animating when the PDF is opened.

EMBED MULTIMEDIA FILES

PDFs have supported multimedia files such as QuickTime movies for some time now, but it has always been a pain because the multimedia files were never really in the PDF. They were linked and you always had to remember to send them separately to your client. The next time you want to make a PDF truly portable, click on the General category on the left-hand side of the Export Adobe PDF dialog; choose Acrobat 6 in the Compatibility pop-up menu in the Options section; and in the Mul-timedia pop-up menu,

select Embed All. The advantage to this is that you'll have one PDF that contains everything. The downside is that the person receiving this PDF will need Adobe Reader 6 or higher (or the full version of Acrobat 6 or higher) to view it.

MAKE INTERACTIVE BUTTONS

PDFs can be interactive and you can use this tip to make buttons that will do things in exported PDFs. For example, if you place a QuickTime movie, you can make a button to alert the recipient of your PDF file that it is a movie that can be played. I would suggest that you create a graphic that looks like a "Play Movie" button and place it near your movie. Use the Button tool to drag a new button around your graphic. Then double-click it with the Selection tool to get to the Button Options dialog. Next, click on the Behaviors button at the top of the dialog and create a behavior that plays the movie upon mouse up. In the Event pop-up menu choose Mouse Up. In the Behavior pop-up menu choose Movie, and you'll see two more pop-up menus appear: one for choosing which movie the button interacts with and another for the Play Options. Once you've set your options, click the Add button and then click OK.

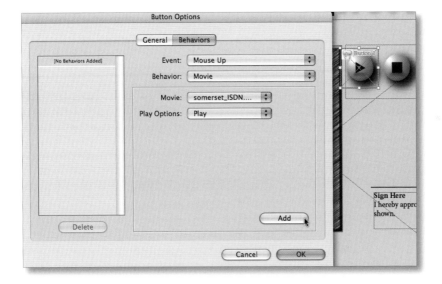

WHEN A STATIC BUTTON IS NOT ENOUGH

Let's take the interactive button tip to a whole new level. Making a button is one thing (see previous tip); making a button rollover is even cooler. If you have an image that you want to be displayed when someone mouses over a button, it can be done. You will need two buttons: the image that you want to appear when someone mouses over the button and the actual button that becomes visible when they mouse over it.

1. Select the image that you want to appear and convert it to a button by choosing Convert to Button from the Object menu's Interactive submenu.

2. Double-click on your newly created graphic button with the Selection tool and name it "over image" in the Button Options dialog. Change the Visibility in PDF pop-up menu to Hidden and click OK.

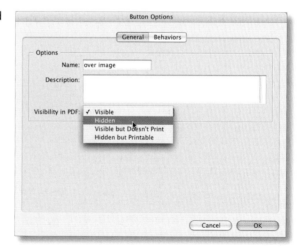

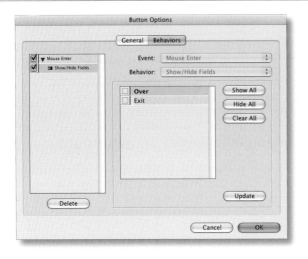

3. Use your Selection tool to double-click on your original button, then click the Behaviors button and add two Behaviors. The first one will be on Mouse Enter and it will show the over image. So change the Event pop-up menu to Mouse Enter and the Behavior pop-up to Show/Hide Fields. Click on the checkbox next to "over image" and then click the Update button.

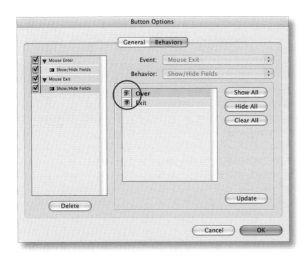

4. The second one should be a Mouse Exit Behavior that will hide the over image. So change the Event pop-up to Mouse Exit and click the checkbox next to "over image" until you have an Eye icon with a red slash through it. Click the Update button, then the OK button. Now when you export to PDF you will have a rollover button.

DEFINE A PDF EXPORT STYLE

Once you have a good set of settings for exporting PDF files, you can use this tip so that you don't have to constantly remember what the settings were and enter them each time: Choose Export from the File menu and Save. When the Export Adobe PDF dialog appears, key in all of your favorite settings for each category. Once you're done, click the Save Preset button, name your preset, and click OK. Your new preset will appear in the Preset pop-up at the top of the Export Adobe PDF dialog.

   USE A PDF EXPORT STYLE

Once you've defined a PDF export style like the one in the previous tip, you can export to a PDF file with those same settings by choosing your saved preset from the Adobe PDF Presets menu under the File menu. The Export Adobe PDF dialog will appear and it will already have all of your settings in it.

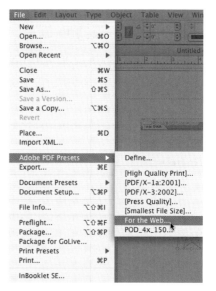

ADD A HOTLINK TO YOUR WEBSITE

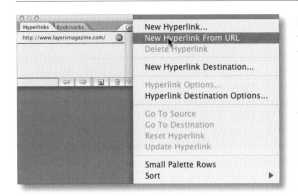

If you're going to export your document to PDF, InDesign can add interactive hyperlinks that will be live in the PDF. If you've already keyed in a valid URL in your document, such as www.macgroup.org, highlight that URL with the Type tool and open the Hyperlinks palette from the Interactive submenu in the Window menu. Then, from the Hyperlinks palette's flyout menu choose New Hyperlink From URL. The hyperlink will be added to the Hyperlinks palette and will automatically be active upon exporting to PDF.

  CREATE A DYNAMIC LINK TO ANOTHER PAGE

Creating hyperlinks to the Web is one thing, but your needs may be as simple as creating a link that merely goes to another page in your PDF. Luckily, InDesign does this automatically when you use the Table of Contents feature. But what about the ones you want to create yourself? Here's a tip that you can use when you want to make your own page links: Go to the page that you want to be able to jump to. Choose New Hyperlink Destination from the Hyperlinks palette's flyout menu. It should default to Page in the Type pop-up menu and give you the page number that you are setting as the destination. Click OK, then go to the page that you want to be able to jump from and select an object or text that people will be able to click on to jump to your destination page. Choose New Hyperlink from the Hyperlinks palette's flyout menu. In the New Hyperlink dialog, name your link if you desire and choose the destination you created from the Name pop-up menu. When you export your PDF, your link will be active. In the General category of the Export Adobe PDF dialog, be sure to check the Hyperlinks checkbox in the Include section.

   RECOGNIZE HYPERLINKS FROM WORD AUTOMATICALLY

You can cut down on some of your work if you're using Microsoft Word as your writing tool for import into InDesign. If you know you want to end up with hyperlinks in your final PDF, you can author them right inside Word. The valid formats are http://www.yoursite.whatever, http://yoursite.whatever, www.yoursite.whatever, and somebody@somedomain.whatever. If you use any of these formats in Word and place the Word document in InDesign, they will automatically be converted into active links.

   GET RID OF THE BLACK BOXES AROUND YOUR LINKS

One side effect of bringing in Word files that contain URLs is that they will appear to have a black box around them onscreen and on the printed page. This is because InDesign defaults to a visible rectangle around links. To avoid this, bring up the Hyperlinks palette (Window>Interactive> Hyperlinks) and double-click one of the imported links in the palette. They are usually called "Hyperlink 1," "Hyperlink 2," etc. In the Hyperlink Options dialog,

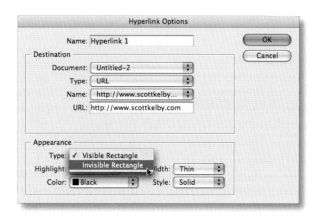

under Appearance, change the Type pop-up menu to Invisible Rectangle. You can do this for each imported hyperlink or, if you have several links, Shift-click to select them all and then perform this operation once to remove the visible rectangle from all of them at once.

USE LAYERS TO GIVE YOUR CLIENT A CHOICE OF CONTENT

If you want to really impress your clients, give them a couple of choices for design or content. Use this tip to create one PDF with multiple choices. It's all about layers! Create three layers and call them "Design 1," "Design 2" and "Design 3." Now assign content to each of the layers. If necessary, you can build other layers on top of these three that will have the same content no matter which design is below. Then turn off the Design 2 and Design 3 layers by clicking on their Eye icons in the Layers palette. From File>Adobe PDF Presets, choose Define and click New. Name your preset and in the Compatibility pop-up menu choose Acrobat 6 (PDF 1.5).

Turn on the option to Create Acrobat Layers in the Options section. Click OK, and then select that preset from the Presets menu in the Adobe PDF Presets dialog. Click Done. When you save your file using this preset, this will make a layered Acrobat 6 (PDF 1.5) compatible file. Anyone with Adobe Reader 6 or higher (or the full version of Acrobat 6 or higher) will be able to turn your layers on or off.

  CREATE BOOKMARKS TO WALK THEM THROUGH YOUR DOCUMENT

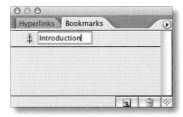

PDF bookmarks have been around almost since day one. However, it's usually a manual task to create them in the full version of Acrobat. Here's a tip on how you can create them right inside of InDesign. Open the Bookmarks palette from the Window menu's Interactive submenu. Go to the page you want to create a bookmark for (we suggest going in order from the beginning of the document to the end) and click the Create New Bookmark icon at the bottom of the Bookmarks palette. This will create a bookmark called "Bookmark." While it's still selected you can rename it right then and there. Do this for each page that you want to bookmark.

CREATE BOOKMARK GROUPS

If you have bookmarks that could be grouped together under one heading, for example, pages in a particular chapter, you can group them together before exporting your PDF. To create a bookmark group, simply drag one bookmark directly on top of another. When it highlights, you can release and it will then indent to the right to indicate that it is now a part of a group.

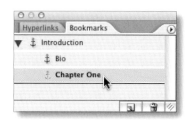

   TRUST NO ONE—PASSWORD PROTECT IT

You don't have to be James Bond to need good document security. If you're sending sensitive information over the Internet, having a secured PDF may help you sleep a little better. Click the Security category in the list down the left-hand side of the Export Adobe PDF dialog. From that window you can check the option Require a Password to Open the Document. Then, in the Document Open Password field enter a password that you will share with the recipient in another communication such as a phone call. When you export your PDF, InDesign will ask you to confirm that you know the password and then you'll be all set.

DON'T GIVE AWAY THE FARM—DISALLOW PRINTING

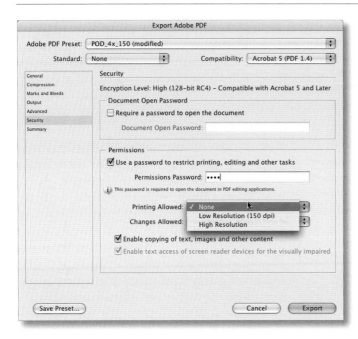

Just because you want to show your customers a proof electronically, that doesn't mean that you want to be taken advantage of. Send them a PDF, but send them one that won't allow them to print. Or send them one that only prints low res. In the Security section of the Export Adobe PDF dialog, there is an option for Use a Password to Restrict Printing, Editing and Other Tasks. Check this box to make the Printing Allowed pop-up menu active. In the Printing Allowed pop-up you can choose among None, Low Resolution (150 dpi), and High Resolution. (Note: The Low Resolution option is not available if you have the PDF compatibility set to Acrobat 4.) Before you export your PDF, choose None and enter a password in the Permissions Password field. The recipient will be able to open and navigate your PDF, but all printing options will be grayed out.

DISALLOW EDITING

Another way of securing a PDF, especially one that you will be posting to your website, is to disallow editing it. This is especially useful for contracts, press releases, and annual reports. Click the Security category in the Export Adobe PDF dialog, check the box for Use a Password to Restrict Printing . . . , and choose None in the Changes Allowed pop-up menu. You will need to give it a Permissions Password and then export your PDF.

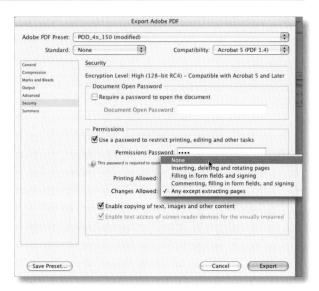

   COMPATIBILITY WITH OLDER VERSIONS OF ACROBAT

It's a fact that not everyone you work with will be upgrading his or her software at the same time that you do. When you need to send someone a PDF and you're not sure which version of Acrobat he has, use the lowest common denominator, Acrobat 4 (PDF 1.3), in the Compatibility pop-up menu of the Options section in the General category of the Export Adobe PDF dialog.

USE SPREADS

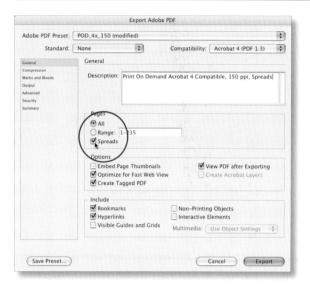

If you've used spreads in your document, chances are that you'll want spreads when you go to PDF. Therefore, all you have to do is check the Spreads checkbox in the Export Adobe PDF dialog. Now your PDF will mimic your InDesign document's side-by-side pages.

  WHAT'S ALL THE BUZZ ABOUT PDF/X?

PDF/X is a subset of PDF designed specifically for printing. It strips out all the whizzbang multimedia, hyperlinks, and other non-print-related baggage in your PDF files. There are two main PDF/X formats: PDF/X-1a and PDF/X-3. PDF/X-1a is for a CMYK (and spot color) only workflow; and PDF/X-3 supports a color-managed workflow, which could include RGB. To create the most print-reliable/print-ready PDF that you can out of InDesign, choose PDF/X-1a: 2001 from the Standard pop-up menu in the Export Adobe PDF dialog.

MAKE IT SMALL BUT KEEP IT LOOKIN' GOOD

We all want the smallest PDF we can get, especially for posting on the Web or for sending via email. However, InDesign's default settings for Screen resolution PDFs can leave a little to be desired for PDFs containing color images, especially if users will be zooming in on them. Our tip for keeping PDFs small, but still looking good, is to start with the Screen preset in the Export Adobe PDF dialog, and then in the Compression category on the left side of the dialog, change the resolution for color images from 72 ppi to 150 ppi. This will make your PDF a little larger, but it will make your photos look a lot better.

    CREATE PDFS WITH TRANSPARENCY

If you have used any of InDesign's transparency effects or placed native Photoshop files with transparency, you have to make a choice when going out to PDF. You have to decide whether to create a flattened PDF or a PDF that supports transparency. By making an Acrobat 4 (PDF 1.3)-compatible PDF, you're taking the transparency flattening into your own hands. However, if you want to maintain the transparency in the PDF, you should create an Acrobat 5 or higher PDF—Acrobat 5 and higher support transparency natively. Flattening will then only take place upon printing.

PLACE INDESIGN PAGES INTO OTHER INDESIGN DOCUMENTS VIA PDF

If you need to bring an InDesign page that you've already created into a new InDesign document, such as an ad or form, a quick way to do so is to export (File>Export) the ad or form as a PDF and then place (File>Place) the PDF in your new document.

Waiting
Tables

WORKING WITH

TABLES

If you're ready for some tear-the-roof-off, go insane, break-all-the-rules, frat-party-gone-wild, uncontrollable good times, then start working in tables. It's off the hook.

Waiting Tables
working with tables

I remember this one night I was at a bachelor party in Vegas. We had a limo and we were hittin' all the clubs up and down the strip, and we wound up at Rain at The Palms. The drinks were flowin', the music was pumpin', lights were flashing, and things were getting a bit crazy out on the dance floor, when all of a sudden, one of my buddies yelled out, "Hey, let's go set some complex tables in InDesign." The next thing you know, we piled back in the limo, headed for the Bellagio's business center, and were setting tables, editing individual cells, and reformatting nested tables until like two in the morning. Suddenly, the cops burst in and one of the SWAT guys pointed a Ruger Mini-14 rifle right at me and screamed, "Any of you boys been filling individual cells with color?" I didn't blink. I just stared at him with that "I just placed an Excel spreadsheet" stare until he decided to stand down, and they finally left. Just another wild night of setting tables in InDesign.

PLACE GRAPHICS IN A TABLE

So you've exhausted all the clever ways of using text in tables and now you want to spice up your tables with graphics. Perhaps you want to do a comparison chart or maybe a catalog page with a graphic next to each description. Although InDesign doesn't have an actual graphics cell, you can 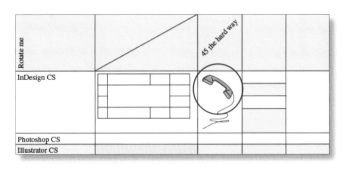 still place graphics into table cells as inline graphics. Simply place your cursor in a table cell with the Type tool and then choose Place from the File menu to find your graphic for placement. Once you place it, InDesign will automatically create a frame for your graphic. You can also copy/cut frames from existing pages and paste them into table cells by selecting your frames with the Type tool, going to Edit>Cut (or Copy), then clicking within your table cell and choosing Edit>Paste.

   GO PLAID, BABY

Liven up your tables with a little color. But rather than simply filling all the cells with the same color, try alternating fills. First, highlight all the cells in your table using the Type tool. Now, either Control-click (PC: Right-click) or choose Table>Table Options>Alternating Fills from the menu bar. In the Table Options dialog you can specify a pattern in the Alternating Patterns pop-up menu, as well as what colors will be used (here we selected Every Other Row filled with blue and white).

FILL INDIVIDUAL CELLS WITH COLOR

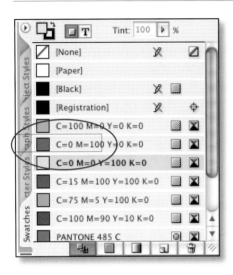

Sometimes you just want to fill a cell with a single color and call it a day. Alternating fills is sweet, but not always necessary. Simply drag a color from your Swatches palette, drop it on any table cell, and the cell will fill with that color. Now you can go home.

   ROTATE TEXT IN TABLES

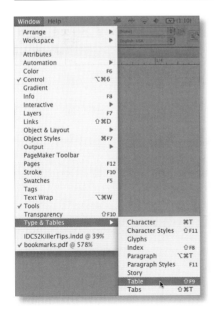

One of the cool ways to make your table stand out is to rotate some of the text. This is especially effective in the headers above the columns. Simply put the cursor in the table cell that you want to rotate and bring up the Table palette from the Window menu in the Type & Tables submenu. Now click the letter "T" icon that represents how you want your text rotated. You may have to increase your row height to accommodate your new choice.

SELECT ROWS AND COLUMNS

One of InDesign's least obvious functions is how you go about selecting rows and columns in a table. Here's how you do it: Choose the Type tool and hover it near the left edge of the table, or near the top of the table if you want to highlight a column. Once you see an arrow pointing to the right or down, click to select the row or column the arrow points to. You can also click-and-drag to select multiple rows or columns at once.

   SELECT THE ENTIRE TABLE

The day has come when you need to select an entire table and modify it all at once. This tip lets you do it in one click. Simply go to the upper-left corner of the first instance of the table and hover the Type tool above the corner until the cursor changes to a diagonal arrow. Now, just click and the entire table will be selected, no matter how many pages it spans.

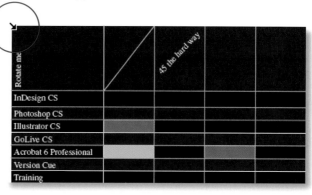

RESIZE ROWS AND COLUMNS

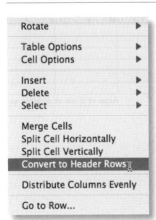

One quick way to resize a single row or column is to simply switch to the Type tool and hover over the line separating two rows or two columns. The cursor should change into a double-arrow pointer. This is the indicator that you can now drag left or right to resize columns, up or down to resize rows.

  RUNNING HEADERS AND FOOTERS

Rotate	▶
Table Options	▶
Cell Options	▶
Insert	▶
Delete	▶
Select	▶
Merge Cells	
Split Cell Horizontally	
Split Cell Vertically	
Convert to Header Rows	
Distribute Columns Evenly	
Go to Row...	

We often like to have headings above each column in a table to identify the contents to the reader. However, if you split up (link) a table from one page to another or even multiple places on the same page, headings don't carry over. This tip is a lifesaver. With the Type tool, highlight the first row or however many rows it takes to contain your header. Now Control-click (PC: Right-click) on the table and choose Convert to Header Rows from the contextual menu. This will place the same header on top of each instance of the table. The same tip works for selecting the last line(s) of the table and choosing Convert to Footer Rows.

PLACE WORD AND EXCEL TABLES

Graphic designers just love getting files from their colleagues who use Microsoft Office products. We especially crave Microsoft Excel documents that need to be laid out in a page-layout program. Well actually, life is about to get a lot better. The next time they ask, "Can I send it to you in Excel?" you can still hem and haw, but say, "Yes!" Choose Place from the File menu and then in the Place dialog point to either an Excel or Word document that contains a table and

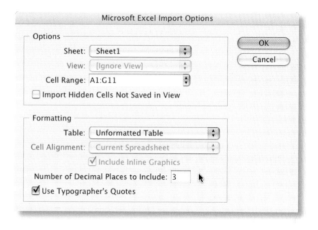

click Open. In the Import Options dialog you can choose options such as importing the table as formatted or unformatted. Once you click OK, all you have to do is place it. InDesign will automatically convert it to an InDesign table. You can still grumble if it makes you feel better.

 CONVERT TEXT TO TABLE

We often get information that needs to be laid out from a database. And while databases have come a long way, they still don't spit out the friendliest types of documents. Ooooohhhh, tab-delimited text, how cool is that? Not! That's okay, go ahead and place it. Now highlight the tab-delimited text with the Type tool and choose Convert Text to Table from the Table menu. Now you've got a table that's a lot more flexible to deal with than just the raw text.

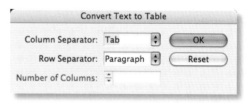

NESTED TABLES

Sometimes creating a table and merging cells together still doesn't give you enough flexibility. So try this tip the next time you need to create a complex table. It's called nested tables. Simply use the Type tool to click your cursor in an existing table cell and choose Insert Table from the Table menu. Now in the Insert Table dialog you can specify the number of rows and columns that you need for the table within a table.

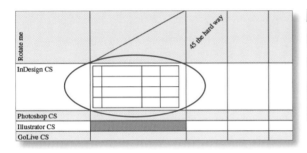 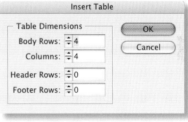

 MAKE BIG ONES OUT OF LITTLE ONES

Instead of trying to cram that large graphic or tons of text into a tiny little table cell, try this tip: Highlight multiple cells with the Type tool and choose Merge Cells from the Table menu.

 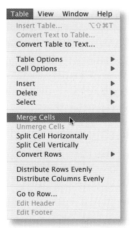

TIME TO SPLIT CELLS

Okay, now it's time to make more cells instead of fewer. Just as you can merge cells together, you can also split them to make more cells. Highlight one or more cells and choose Split Cell Horizontally or Split Cell Vertically from the Table menu.

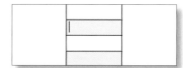

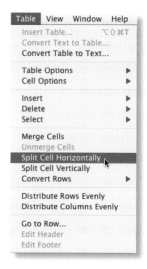

   REMOVE THE TABLE STROKE

One of the first things that people want to do after setting up their table is to get rid of the lines between the rows and columns. Actually it's easier than you think. InDesign uses the same stroke metaphor for tables that it uses for everything else. To get rid of a stroke, highlight the rows and columns and from the Color or the Stroke palette choose None for color or zero for the stroke weight.

INSERT A ROW AT THE END WITH A TAB

You need to add one more row at the end of the table because someone (usually the customer) decided to add "one more thing." No problem, simply use the Type tool to put your cursor in the last cell of the table and (here it comes) press the Tab key on the keyboard. That will automatically add a row onto the end of your table.

  INSERT ROWS AND COLUMNS

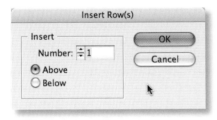

Creating a table with eight rows and four columns sounded like a great idea at the time, but now you need to add another row in the middle of the table to key in some information that you forgot. Use this tip to add as many rows or columns as you want. With the Type tool, put your cursor in a row either above or below where you want to insert more rows. Now choose Insert>Row from the Table menu. You will get a dialog asking how many rows you want and whether you want to insert them above or below the row you have selected. This tip works the same way if you put your cursor in a column and choose Insert>Column from the Table menu.

BRING ORDER TO TABLE CHAOS!

So you've become a junkie for dragging the width and height of your columns and rows all willy-nilly? Now you've decided you want nice evenly spaced rows and columns. So use this tip next time to bring everything back to order. Use the Type tool to highlight the rows or columns in which you want to distribute the space evenly. Now choose either Distribute Rows Evenly or Distribute Columns Evenly from the Table menu. Like magic, the space in your rows and columns will be evenly spaced.

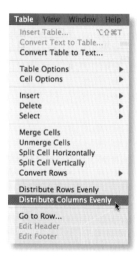

   LINE UP AND FLY RIGHT

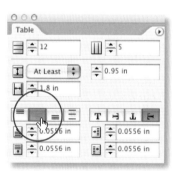

At this point you're probably a pro at putting text in cells. Now how about aligning it? The cool part is that you do it the same way you align text that's not in a cell. Simply select the cells with the Type tool and choose your options from the Control palette or from the Paragraph palette. If you want text aligned in the center of the cell, you can do that from the Control or Table palette (Window>Type & Tables>Table).

CREATE DIAGONAL LINES

I don't quite understand why, but you might want to have diagonal lines in your table cells. Rather than painstakingly drawing them one by one, you can have InDesign draw them for you. Highlight the cells where you need them and choose Diagonal Lines from the Cell Options submenu under the Table menu. You can choose a diagonal line that leans to the left, right, or both. How exciting! If only Adobe had seen fit to allow your text to be rotated to match the angle, you would really be in good shape.

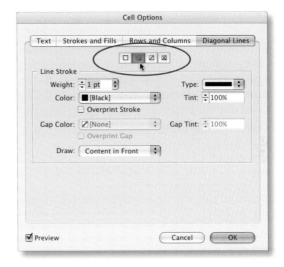

   ANGLED TEXT? MAKE IT SO

That last tip may have left you obsessed with having text on an angle in a table cell. Give it up; the feature just isn't there. However, you can fake it by rotating the text first and then pasting the rotated text into the cell. Create a small text frame with the Type tool, type your text, and then use the Rotate tool to rotate it to whatever degree you like. Then select the frame with the Selection tool and cut it (Mac: Command-X [PC: Control-X]). Now simply click with the Type tool into the cell where you want it and paste it in (Mac: Command-V [PC: Control-V]). It's not perfect, but it works!

   IT JUST WON'T FIT

Hey, guess what? It won't fit and nobody likes reading 4-point type—so stop trying to cram that big table at the bottom of your page. Place your table where you want it to be and then collapse the bottom of the frame by clicking on the frame's bottom center handle and dragging up with the Selection tool until it fits on the 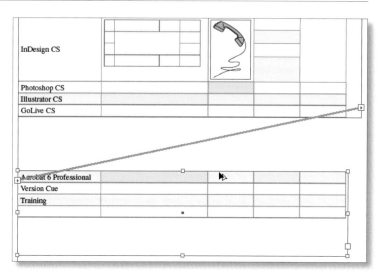 page. Now you should have a red plus sign on the bottom right. Click the plus sign and continue placing your table on the next page. You'll make your readers a lot happier.

Blue Prints

PRINTING AND THE CREATIVE SUITE

So how do tips on printing and on working with other Creative Suite applications belong in the same chapter? Do you want some fluffy-sounding run-around answer

Blue Prints
printing and the Creative Suite

or do you want the truth? Believe me, I can make it sound pretty compelling if you're up for the fluff answer. No? You want the truth? Okay, I'm going to give it to you straight, but if I tell the absolute truth, it's understood that you won't hold it against us in any way. Deal? Deal. Here's the thing: We had enough printing tips to easily fill a chapter, but we were short on the "Suite" tips. Although we originally planned on having an entire "Working with the Creative Suite" chapter, we just couldn't come up with enough tips, so we had to bury our Creative Suite tips within some other chapter. The type and layout chapters were so long we couldn't add them there, and although the tips were pretty good, they weren't really cool enough for the way-cool tips chapter; so basically they ended up here. Hey, you said you wanted the truth, but now that you've heard it, admit it—you wish you had asked for the fluffy compelling-sounding reason. See, this is what they mean by "The truth hurts."

PRINT TO DIFFERENT PRINTERS WITH EASE

It's not uncommon for people to have two or more printers these days. Each printer, of course, has its own way of working and its own driver and its own settings. Rather than having to remember which settings you used the last time, use saved Print Presets. Choose File>Print Presets>Define and click New in the Print Presets dialog. Now you can choose a printer and all the settings you want for that printer. Name your settings and click OK. The next time you want to print with those settings, simply choose your setting from the File menu's Print Presets submenu (as shown below, left). The Print dialog will appear and your settings will already be in place. All you have to do is hit Print.

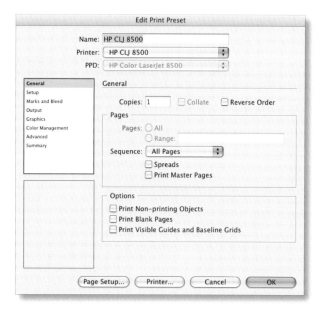

AVOID SEPARATION SURPRISES ON PRESS

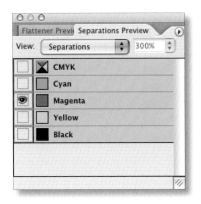

If you'll be color-separating your InDesign file, there's a way to get a preview of your results before the actual separation to film (or plates) occurs—which is helpful in avoiding costly surprises on press. Just go under the Window menu, under Preview, and choose Separations Preview to bring up the Separations Preview palette (as shown here). From the palette's View pop-up menu, choose Separations and then you can view individual plates by turning their visibility on/off using the Eye icons (just as you would in the Layers palette).

   ## HOW MANY PLATES DO YOU REALLY HAVE?

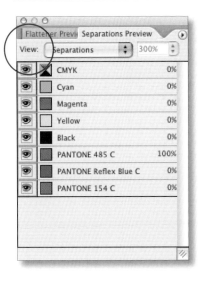

More often than we'd like to admit we may create a job with more colors than we anticipated. This is usually done by accident and can be a real pain in the butt to track down. Here's a tip that will make your day: Choose Window>Output>Separations Preview. Then just as in the previous tip, choose Separations from the View pop-up menu at the top of the Separations Preview palette. This will show you how many plates your job uses. You can find that rogue plate by simply hiding all the other plates by clicking on the Eye icons.

USE THE INK MANAGER TO ELIMINATE ROGUE PLATES

Sometimes you end up with extra plates in your job due to colors that come in from placed graphics. The color is the same as one that you have already defined, but it has a different name. You can fix this using the Ink Manager. You can access the Ink Manager either from the Separations Preview palette's flyout menu or in the Output panel of the Print dialog. Click the color that you want to alias to another existing color in the Ink Manager dialog. Then

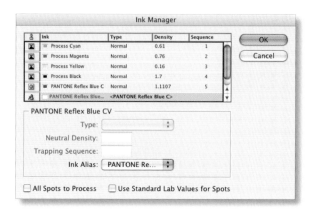

choose the second color in the Ink Alias pop-up menu. Any objects using this extra color will now be on the plate of the ink that you choose to alias.

   PREFLIGHT FOR THE MOST COMMON PROBLEMS

After you send a job out to be printed, the only time you want to hear from the printer is to know that the job is done. So check for the most common mistakes before you burn your CD or FTP your files. Choose Preflight from the File menu and InDesign will automatically run through your entire document looking for missing fonts, broken links, missing fonts placed in vector graphics, extra color plates, and graphics using the RGB color space.

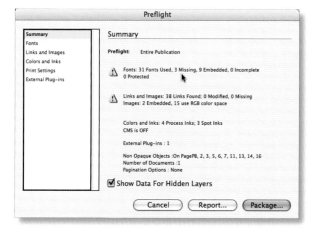

PREFLIGHT: SHOW PROBLEMS ONLY

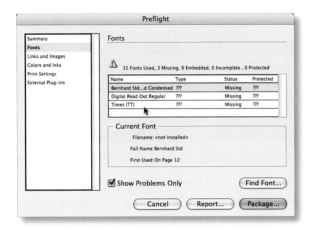

When I'm looking at my Preflight results I really don't care about what's right. I care about what's wrong! In each of the Preflight panels, there is an option to Show Problems Only. If you check that box Preflight will list only the problems in any of the respective panels.

   ## PACKAGE IT UP

Although many people have moved to a PDF workflow, there are still many printers out there that want to work with the native files. You've placed graphics from all over your hard drive, you've used various fonts, and you don't want to have to go gathering up all that stuff manually. Well there is a solution for this: Choose Package from the File menu. The great thing about this is that it will automatically run Preflight too, so if you know you're going to package the document, you don't have to run Preflight manually. The Package feature copies all of the InDesign document, the links, and even the fonts to a location/folder of your choice. Then all you have to do is Stuff it, Zip it, FTP it, or burn it to a CD and transport it to your printer.

NON-PRINTING OBJECTS—PRINT THEM ANYWAY

Okay, so you've defined objects in your document as non-printing, but now you want to print them anyway. Rather than going back through the document and one by one making them printable again, just click the Print Non-Printing Objects box in the Options section of the Print dialog. This way, you won't miss any, and you won't have to worry about making them non-printing again.

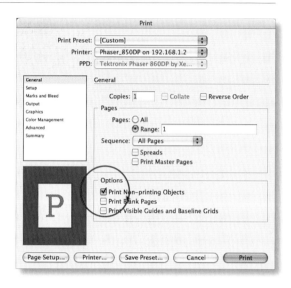

 CYCLE THROUGH YOUR PRINT SETTINGS

It's not a print preview, but it's the next best thing. When you want to see the current settings for printing your document, simply click the box where you see the big "P" in the lower left of the Print dialog. Each time you click inside the box it will cycle to your next print setting, as shown here.

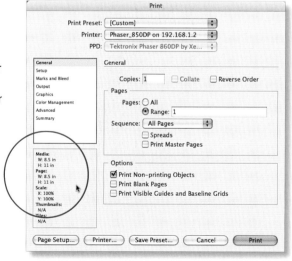

SWITCH PRINTERS ON THE FLY

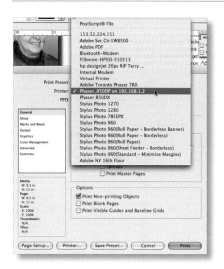

Mac users, the Chooser is gone. This is a good thing because you can now switch printers in any Mac OS X-native application's Print dialog. InDesign's Print dialog also has one extra choice that you may not have noticed. It's the Print Preset pop-up menu. So if you've created a print preset that you wanted to choose from the File menu, but you chose Print by mistake, don't cancel; just choose it from the Print Preset pop-up and you're ready to go.

   SPEED UP PRINTING

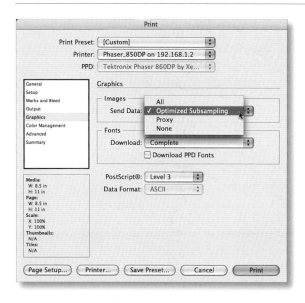

When you print from InDesign you probably want the fastest, most accurate printing you can get, right? To speed things up, switch to the Graphics category of the Print dialog and make sure that the Send Data pop-up menu in the Images section is set to Optimized Subsampling. This option will send down only as much data as your printer can handle. For example, if you had a 1,200-dpi image and you had only a 600-dpi printer, sending down 1,200 dpi would be a waste of time. Optimized Subsampling sends only the right amount of image data.

PRINT PANEL NAVIGATION SHORTCUT

The Print dialog has several panels for choosing your print options. Here's a tip to let you cycle through them quickly. Simply use your Up and Down Arrow keys on your keyboard to take you through the various panels.

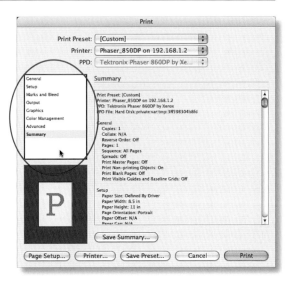

 CHANGE YOUR LINE SCREEN WHEN GOING MONOCHROME

Not everyone can afford four-color printing. There are folks out there still using monochrome printers and making plates from laser prints or even running copies on a copier. You can vary the line screen that will be used on your monochrome printer. Choose the Output panel on the left of the Print dialog and change the Color pop-up menu to Composite Gray and then change the Screening pop-up menu to Custom. You'll notice that now you can enter your own Frequency (lines per inch) as well as an Angle (although 45° will work for most folks).

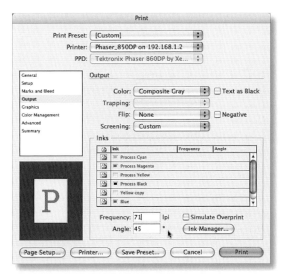

PRINT SEPARATIONS LIKE A PRO

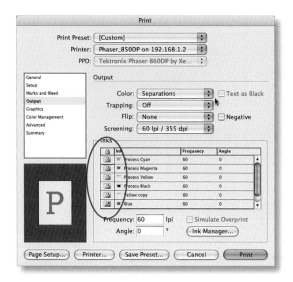

By default InDesign prints color in Composite mode. If you're printing to your color printer, that's what you want. However, if you're printing to an image setter or plate maker, chances are you want a separate plate or piece of film for each color. Switch to the Output panel in the Print dialog and choose Separations from the Color pop-up menu. In the Inks section you will be able to manually turn on and off which plates you want to print by clicking on the tiny printer icons on the left.

   ## PRINT THE SLUG

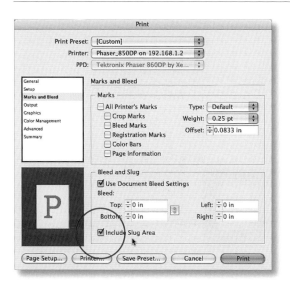

When you create an InDesign document you have the option of creating a slug area. This area is typically used by ad agencies and designers to place information about the job and its print settings. In the Marks and Bleed category in the Print dialog, go to the Bleed and Slug section, where you have the option whether to Include Slug Area when you print the document. It's off by default.

ACCESS PRINTER-SPECIFIC FEATURES

Unfortunately InDesign's Print dialog may not include every single option that is available in your printer driver. For example, our Tektronix Phaser 850DP can do duplexing, but those controls aren't in the InDesign Print dialog. When you want to access all of the options available to your printer, click the Printer button at the bottom of the Print dialog. This will allow you to access the normal OS-level printer driver to enable the options that InDesign is missing.

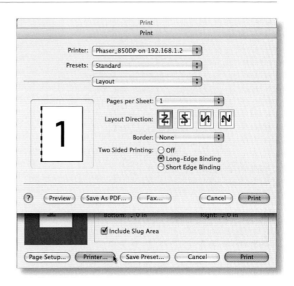

    DOWNLOAD PPD FONTS ANYWAY!

You used Times Roman and it's coming out Courier. How can this be? Times Roman is built into the printer. If you have fonts that are built into the printer but they're not printing right, switch to the Graphics panel of the Print dialog (yeah, I know that's the first place you'd look, right?); and for the Fonts option enable the checkbox for Download PPD Fonts. This will force InDesign to download the fonts that should be in the printer anyway.

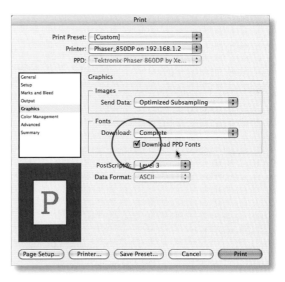

SCALE PAGES TO FIT YOUR MEDIA SIZE

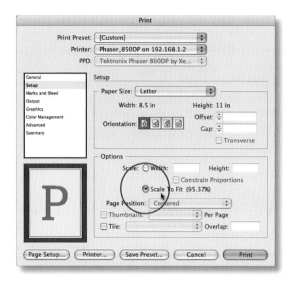

If you have something that was designed for a large page and need to shrink it down to fit the media that you're currently printing to, this tip will save you time. Rather than scale the objects in the document, simply choose Scale To Fit in the Setup panel of the Print dialog and print your job.

   WHEN YOUR SERVICE PROVIDER WON'T TAKE AN INDESIGN FILE

If your printer or service provider flat-out refuses to accept InDesign files, smack 'em. Okay, maybe that's not a good idea. Work around the problem. In most cases, they would probably accept a PDF. If not, you can export the pages as EPS files or even print PostScript. If your printer/service provider isn't open to any of these options, it may be time to move to another printer/service provider. At http://partners.adobe.com you can find print houses that are eagerly accepting InDesign files.

PULL THE PLUG ON AUTO-UPDATING

If Adobe comes out with a free maintenance update for InDesign, they really want you to have it (read as: really, really, really!). That's why they've included a feature that goes to Adobe's website and checks for updates automatically. This auto-check feature is actually pretty helpful and these updates are designed to make your work easier by fixing bugs or other potential problems; but some people just hate the fact that it goes out and searches without their specifically asking it to. If you're one of those people (you know who you are), then go under the InDesign menu (PC: Edit menu), under Preferences, and choose Updates. When the Preferences dialog appears, uncheck Automatically Check for Updates Every Month. From that point on, it's up to you to check for updates from Adobe, and if you know that in reality you're likely to forget (like us), you may not want to turn this feature off after all.

 ## PLACE NATIVE PHOTOSHOP FILES

Although TIFF files are still the norm, they're not the most convenient to work with. Chances are that you have used layers in creating your Photoshop artwork. In making a TIFF you would probably do a Save As to create a flattened TIFF and now you have two files to deal with. Instead of making TIFFs just place (File>Place) the native Photoshop document. InDesign will automatically flatten it in the print stream.

PLACE NATIVE ILLUSTRATOR FILES

InDesign works with Illustrator in two ways. You can either copy and paste vector paths from Illustrator into InDesign or you can place (File>Place) native Illustrator files. The advantage of copying and pasting vector paths is that they are converted to InDesign vectors and can be modified in InDesign. The disadvantage is that there is no link back to the original Illustrator drawing. The advantage of placing native Illustrator files is that you maintain all the effects and transparency and a link back to the original .AI file. However, placed Illustrator files cannot be modified in InDesign.

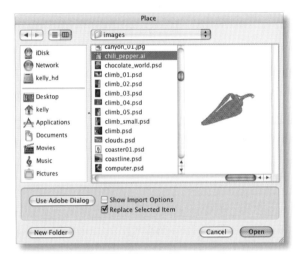

   SHARE COLOR SETTINGS WITH PHOTOSHOP AND ILLUSTRATOR

InDesign, Photoshop, and Illustrator all share the same color management settings. Therefore, when you've spent time getting color right in Photoshop, InDesign can use those same settings. Choose Color Settings from the Edit menu. Click Load, and choose the custom color settings you created and named in Photoshop. If you didn't create custom settings, then simply match the settings that you used in the other apps for consistent color in all three programs.

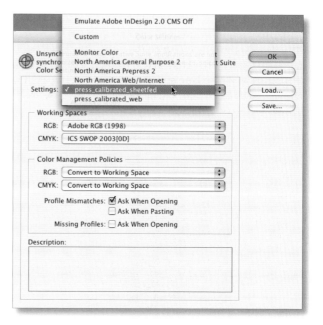

EDIT YOUR GRAPHICS AND HAVE THEM AUTO-UPDATE

If you're working with placed graphics created in either Adobe Photoshop or Adobe Illustrator (and our guess is you are) you can edit a placed image directly by holding the Option key (PC: Alt key) and double-clicking on the image. This opens the image in the application that created it (Photoshop or Illustrator) so you can edit the image as you'd like. (You can also Control-click [PC: Alt-click] your image and choose Edit Original, as shown here.) When you resave the images after your edits and return to InDesign, these edited images will automatically be updated in your InDesign document. Mighty cool.

   GOING FROM PRINT TO THE WEB?

If the boss comes by and says something like, "That new brochure design looks great! Can we get a version up on the Web?" your first reaction might be to create a PDF (which in many cases is the right reaction), but what if you want a standard HTML webpage instead? If you're using Adobe GoLive as your Web authoring application, InDesign can make your conversion much easier. Just go under the File menu and choose Package For GoLive. Though InDesign will let you save the package anywhere you like, it makes it a whole lot easier if you save it to the InDesignPackages folder located in your GoLive site's web-data folder. After you choose a location to save your "package," you'll be greeted with a dialog (shown here) that offers options such as the ability to package all—or just a portion—of your document. Click the Package button, and you're ready to open your file (and images) in GoLive for further editing.

New Attitude

WHAT'S NEW
IN INDESIGN
CS2

There's nothing like cracking open a new piece of software, going through the arduous installation process, waiting with bated breath, only to see what appears at first

New Attitude
what's new in InDesign CS2

glance to be the same old interface. Believe it or not, that's a good thing. Imagine the panic in the streets and rioting in San Jose if every time someone installed an upgrade everything was totally different and moved around just for the sake of making things different and moving things around. Although InDesign CS2 looks a lot like InDesign CS, there's a lot of new stuff in there. In this chapter we'll take you through the new features that matter most. You'll be up and running in no time, thumbing your nose at those poor misfortunate souls who are still working the way they always did since InDesign 2 and not taking advantage of the things you're about to learn. You could read this chapter and then hold a class for everyone, but that's so not like you.

DRAG-AND-DROP FROM THE BRIDGE

Whether you bought InDesign CS2 as a stand-alone application or as part of the Adobe Creative Suite 2, you also received an additional application called Adobe Bridge. The Bridge is neat because it allows you to see a folder full of images without having to open them up one by one. Here's a tip for laying out your next job faster. Use the Bridge to navigate to the folder containing all the assets you need to place in your layout. Then simply drag the images from the Bridge directly onto your InDesign page. You can either drag images into existing frames or let InDesign create the frames for you on the fly. You can even drag multiple images at once and then sort them out once they are on the page.

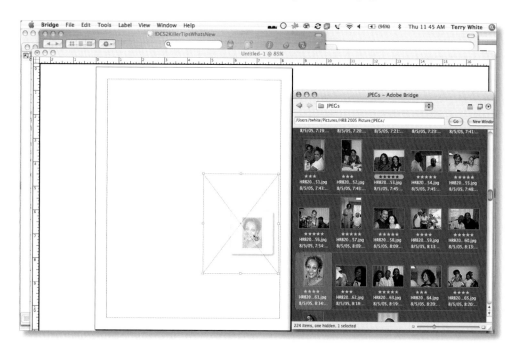

OPEN THE BRIDGE FROM INDESIGN

Using Adobe Bridge is like having your own image palette accessible anytime you need it. However, finding and launching the Bridge can be a pain. But there are a couple of easy ways to access the Bridge directly from InDesign CS2. The first way is

to choose Browse from the File menu, or use the keyboard shortcut: Command-Option-O (PC: Control-Alt-O). The second way is to simply click the Go To Bridge button right on the Control bar.

    PLACE A STOCK PHOTO COMP IMAGE

With the Bridge you can search the world's leading stock photography houses. When you find a stock image you like and you want to test it in your layout, the Bridge allows you to download a low-res comp image. Rather than trying to find that image later via the Place command, simply drag it in from the downloaded comps area of the Bridge. Just drag the thumbnail from the Bridge to your existing frame or directly to your page in InDesign.

   PURCHASE A STOCK PHOTO IMAGE FROM INDESIGN

Which images are yours and which are stock photo comps? That may be a question that comes to mind after you've started placing lots of stock photo comps mixed in with your own images. This tip will not only make it easy for you to tell which images are which, but it will also allow you to go ahead and purchase the images you need. If you do decide to purchase an image, it will automatically download and replace the comp image. Simply bring up your InDesign Links palette. You'll see all the links in your document. The stock photo comps will have a small film negative icon on them to the right of the name of the link. That's a dead giveaway that will tell you which links are stock photo comps and which ones aren't. In order to purchase an image, simply select Purchase This Image from the Links palette flyout menu.

 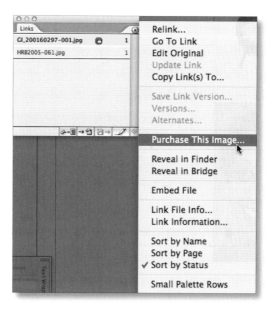

SNIPPETS

Almost everyone is familiar with InDesign Libraries, right? You know, those palettes that you can create by choosing New > Library from the File menu. Once one is open, you can drag-and-drop page elements into it. As long as you keep that library open (or even if you open it later), you can drag elements from it onto other InDesign pages in the same document or other documents. Now imagine if these elements weren't tied to an InDesign Library? That's where Snippets come in. The next time you want to use elements from one InDesign document in another InDesign document, simply drag the elements to the desktop or a Bridge window and it will create an XML-based Snippet that can be used in any other InDesign page or document. You can even email Snippets. It's like having Library elements without the Library file.

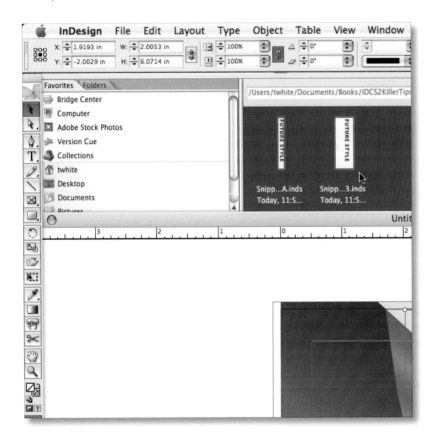

WYSIWYG FONT MENUS

Choosing between different fonts is a daily exercise in the page layout world. It's pretty cool that you can just start typing the name of the font that you want to get to in the Control palette. But what if you're not sure which font you want to use until you see it? Now you can simply choose the Font menu (under the Type menu) and not only will it show you the names of the fonts, but it will also show you what type of font it is and provide a sample of what the font looks like. If it's an OpenType font it will have an "O" to the left of the font's name. An "a" denotes a PostScript Type 1 font, and a "TT" means it's a TrueType font. So if your service provider wants you to avoid TrueType fonts, you can easily do that by scanning the list and avoiding those font types.

   DRAG-AND-DROP TEXT

When you highlight text in an InDesign document and start dragging the Type tool across it again, by default it will simply make a new selection. If you want the behavior to change so that you can drag-and-drop your highlighted text, try this tip: Choose Type from the Preferences menu and check Enable in Layout View from the Drag and Drop Text Editing section. Now, if you use the Type tool and hover over highlighted text on the page, you'll notice that there is a little pointer with a "T". You can now drag that highlighted text to another location either in the same frame or a different frame.

DYNAMIC SPELLING

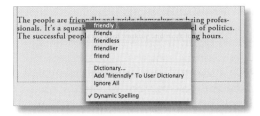

I've used Microsoft Word for years and years, mainly because it has one thing that I really like: Dynamic Spelling. I like having my spelling checked as I type. In InDesign CS2, this is now a built-in capability. However, it's off by default. You can enable it by choosing Dynamic Spelling from the Spelling menu (under the Edit menu). Any words in your document that are not in the dictionary will be underlined in red. You can then Control-click (PC: Right-click) on them to bring up a list of suggested words that InDesign thinks you're trying to spell.

 AUTOCORRECT

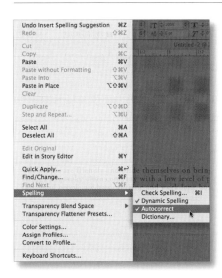

If you're not the world's most accurate typist, you'll love Autocorrect. Autocorrect is off by default in InDesign. However, if you enable it (choose Autocorrect from the Spelling menu under the Edit menu) and type a commonly misspelled word —such as "teh"— InDesign will correct it as "the". You can even add your own Autocorrect words by going to the Autocorrect preferences (in the Preferences dialog) and adding them.

   MULTIPLE USER DICTIONARIES

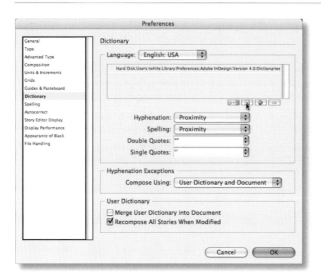

InDesign CS2 documents can now be spell checked against multiple dictionaries simultaneously. So you can spell check using the user dictionary that you normally add words to, and you can also choose additional dictionaries, such as a dictionary of corporate terms, from the Dictionary preferences. Or, if you want to create a new dictionary altogether, you can do that by adding it in the Dictionary preferences.

   IMPORT TEXT FILES TO THE DICTIONARY

If you work in a workgroup where everyone uses InDesign, here's a tip to increase the speed and consistency of your spell checking. Type a list of words that are specific to your kind of work, such as technical terms, acronyms, etc. Then export or save that list as a text file (.txt). Choose Dictionary from the Spelling menu (under the Edit menu) and click the Import button to select the text file you created. After each user does this, you will all have the same words in your user dictionaries—plus the words you've already added.

FOOTNOTES

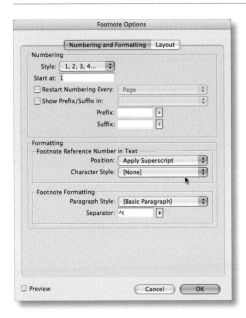

Stop building your footnotes manually! InDesign CS2 has an automatic footnote capability. That's not really the tip, though. The tip is that not only can you choose Insert Footnote from the Type menu, you can also control how that footnote looks using style sheets: Choose Document Footnote Options from the Type menu and assign a Character Style to your Footnote Reference Number and a Paragraph Style to your Footnote Formatting.

 PASTE WITHOUT FORMATTING

InDesign tries to do the right thing by pasting text exactly as it was formatted in the source document. However, this can be frustrating when you're just trying to paste raw text that you want to format yourself. This tip will end the frustration. Copy your text from any application (such as Microsoft Word) and then choose Paste Without Formatting from the Edit menu in InDesign CS2. Your text will be pasted as raw text that you can then stylize however you'd like.

OVERSET TEXT IN THE STORY EDITOR

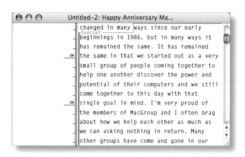

A question that has plagued desktop publishers since day one is this: "How much text is left to place?" The next time you place text in a frame and you get the red plus sign indicating that there is more text, try this tip to know exactly where you stand. Put your cursor on the last line of text that's showing in the frame. Then bring up that text in the Story Editor by choosing Edit in Story Editor from the Edit menu. Now you'll see your overset text, indicated by a red vertical line.

FRAME-BASED BASELINE GRIDS

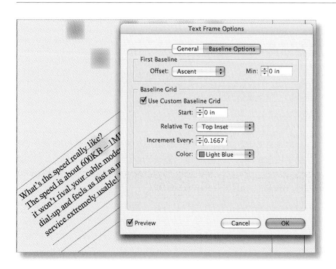

Baseline grids have been around for years, working behind the scenes on your pages to keep your columns of text even across the page. However, the functionality of a baseline grid completely falls apart if you have text in a frame and the frame needs to be rotated. The text can't line up to the page's baseline grid if the frame is on an angle. If you find yourself in this situation, try this tip. First, you have to create your text and align it to the grid by clicking the Align to Baseline Grid button in the Paragraph options of the Control palette. You'll probably also want to Show the Baseline Grid in the View menu (under Grids & Guides). Once your text is aligned in the frame, that's when you can go ahead and rotate the frame.

PHOTOSHOP LAYER CONTROLS

InDesign has always been able to place native Photoshop files. However, you were only able to get the current state of the Photoshop layers. (In other words, if a Photoshop file had three layers but only two were turned on, you'd only get those two layers when you placed the file.) Now you can actually turn the layers on and off of a placed Photoshop file directly in InDesign. If the Photoshop file contains Layer Comps (groups of layers turned on and off) you can control those, too. Place a native Photoshop file that contains at least two layers. With the image selected on the page choose Object Layer Options (from the Object menu). You'll then be able to turn layers on and off for that one instance of the placed Photoshop file. Be sure to enable the Preview checkbox so that you can see the updates live. This tip also works for placed PDF files that contain layers.

OBJECT STYLES

Paragraph and character style sheets have been around almost as long as desktop publishing itself. They allow you to quickly format paragraphs and individual character selections. Up until now, style sheets only applied to text. But what about your objects? The frames that you place your text and images into can contain attributes such as transparency settings, strokes, number of columns, etc. We've always had to set these attributes one-by-one in the past. With this tip, you can streamline your workflow. Create or select a frame already on the page. Give it whatever attributes you want, such as a stroke and a drop shadow. Then bring up the Object Styles palette and click the Create New Style button at the bottom. This will create a new Object Style that contains those attributes. You can then select other frames in your document and simply click on your new Object Style to assign it to the frames you selected.

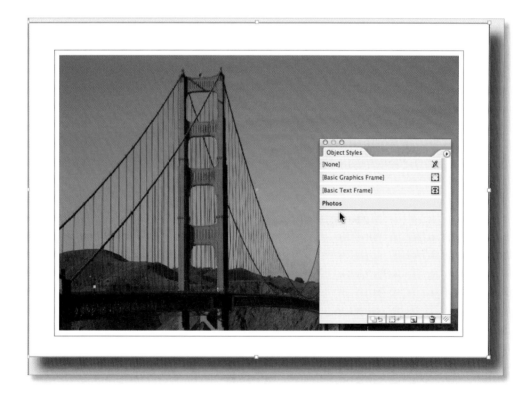

SELECTIVELY LOAD STYLES

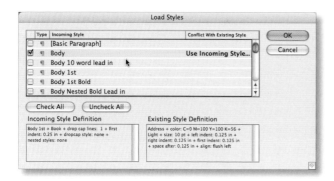

You spent time creating this really cool style sheet in the document you worked on last week and now you need to use it in your new document. The problem is that the document you already created has about a million other style sheets that you don't need in the new document. There is a solution! You can selectively load styles from one InDesign document into another. Open or create the new document and then bring up the style palette for the styles that you want to import. For example, bring up the Paragraph Styles palette and then choose Load Paragraph Styles from the flyout menu. You'll get a dialog box asking you to choose the document from which you want to import styles. Now you have the option to choose just the styles you want to import.

   ## QUICK APPLY

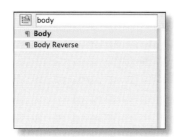

Have you ever caught yourself digging for the right style palette? You can see the Paragraph Styles palette, but the Character Styles and Object Styles palettes don't jump out at you. What if you could apply styles without having the palettes open at all? Use this tip to quickly apply paragraph, character, or object styles depending on what you have selected on the page: Press Command-Return (PC: Control-Return) to bring up the Quick Apply palette. Type in the name of the style you want to apply. Once it's highlighted you can simply press Return to apply the style and the palette goes away.

● **APPLY NEXT STYLE**

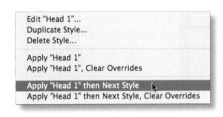

When you create a Paragraph Style you have the option to choose a Next Style. That means that, when you hit Return, InDesign automatically switches to another style that you've assigned as the Next Style. For example, if after typing a headline you always type the author's name, you could set up a Next Style where the Author style immediately follows the Headline style. Catchy, huh? This works great as long as you're typing directly into InDesign. If you're placing text, use this tip to apply all of your Paragraph Styles at once: Highlight all the text that you want to apply the styles to, then Control-click (PC: Right-click) on the first style you want to apply. You'll get a contextual menu that allows you to apply the style you clicked on, as well as the Next Style that you've defined. This effect will ripple through the rest of the highlighted text, applying all your Next Styles.

   RESET TO BASE STYLE

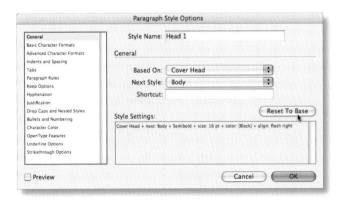

If the style sheet you're creating is getting out of hand and you want to reset it back to the base settings, bring up the style definition and press the Reset To Base button to quickly restore the original attributes in a new style you're specifying or editing.

CLEAR OVERRIDES

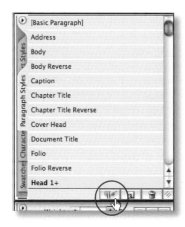

When applying paragraph styles, sometimes the paragraph you're applying it to may have some local overrides, with certain words being bold, italicized, or maybe even a different font. In previous versions of InDesign, the tip would be to hold down the Option key and click the style to override this individual formatting. You can still do it that way in InDesign CS2, but now there is also a new button at the bottom of the Paragraph Styles and Object Styles palettes that will do the trick: Place your cursor in the paragraph with the overrides that you want to clear and press the Clear Overrides button.

ALIGN AWAY/TOWARDS SPINE

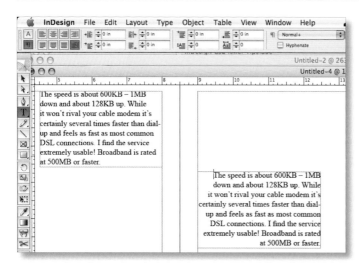

You can align text using a variety of different options, such as Align Left, Align Center, Align Right, Justified, etc. The next time you want to align text based on its location in relation to the spine, try this tip: Put your cursor in the paragraph that you want to align toward or away from the spine and go to the Paragraph options in the Control palette. There you will find one button to align your text toward the spine and one to align your text away from the spine. In the image here, you can see that the text is set to align away from the spine, and it automatically shifts to align left or right depending on what side of the spine it's on.

WORD IMPORT

If you're in the page layout world, receiving Word files from people is a fact of life. InDesign can place Word files pretty easily. By default, they come in as they were formatted in Word. However, if you want to control exactly how the text comes in, choose Place from the File menu and make sure you check the Show Import Options checkbox. Now choose a Word file to place and you'll get a dialog box that lets you control just about every aspect of how the file is formatted as it is imported. You can choose to accept or discard the formatting already in place. Also, don't forget to check out the Customize Style Import option at the bottom of the dialog, which allows you to map the incoming Word styles to your InDesign styles.

FILL FRAME PROPORTIONALLY

I gotta say that the new Fill Frame Proportionally command is probably my favorite new "little thing I love about InDesign." As you know, when you create a frame in InDesign and then place an image into it, there's a strong chance that the proportions are not going to match. When you use the Fit Content Proportionally command, there will inevitably be some space left over on either the right side or the bottom. This is fine if you need to see 100% of the image. However, if it's a photo where the edges can be cropped, then you will probably scale it manually to fit the frame perfectly. (It's the true perfectionist in you showing through.) Next time, use this tip: Place your photo and instead of using Fit Content Proportionally, use Fill Frame Proportionally. This will fill the frame completely without distorting or stretching the image. InDesign may have to do some cropping to achieve this, but you can always use the Direct Selection tool to reposition the image if necessary.

ANCHORED OBJECTS

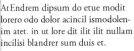

Go beyond simple inline graphics with Anchored Objects. Yeah, it may sound like a marketing pitch, but this is a really useful tip. If you need your graphics to move along with your text—whether it be inside or, better yet, outside the text frame—try the following: Insert your cursor in the text that the graphic is related to. Then choose Insert from the Anchored Object menu (under the Object menu). This will present you with a dialog box with numerous options for the placement of the object frame in relation to the anchor inside the text. One option I would recommend is Relative to Spine, which automatically aligns your object to the left or right of the text frame depending on which side of the spine it's on. This is key in book and magazine publishing.

 TRANSFORM AGAIN

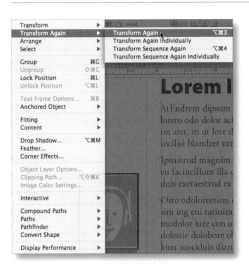

Sometimes you get something just right on the first try. Don't you wish you could just tell InDesign to "do it again?" That's what Transform Again lets you do. If you move or rotate an object, you can select other objects that you want moved or rotated in the same fashion. Go to Transform Again (under the Object menu) and choose Transform Again Individually. The objects that you selected will be transformed just like the last object. If you want the selected objects to be transformed as a group, you can do that, too, by choosing Transform Again.

SHAPE CONVERSIONS

Drawing that circle sounded like a great idea—at first. Now you wish that it were a rectangle instead. Don't delete it and start over. Convert it instead. You can convert the shape of a frame to a different shape by choosing Convert Shape from the Object menu and choosing the shape you need.

DROP SHADOW NOISE & SPREAD OPTIONS

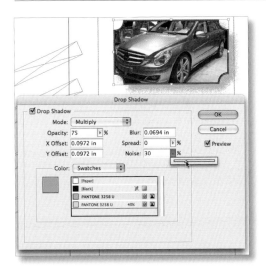

You can have a lot of fun in InDesign creating drop shadows and feathering objects, including text frames. However, until now the drop shadow options were pretty basic. There is a design effect that I refer to as "grunge"; you see it everywhere in design today. Now you can create those grungy, noisy kinds of drop shadows directly in InDesign. Select an object on the page and choose Drop Shadow from the Object menu. You'll notice that you now have options for Spread and Noise. Spread controls the amount of softness from the object to the edge of the shadow, and Noise does just what it sounds like it would do: it adds noise to the shadow itself.

   IMPORT MULTI-PAGE PDFS

Placing PDF files into InDesign gives you the added flexibility of repurposing content to use in a different layout. However, it would be a pain to place a multi-page PDF one page at a time. The next time you want to place a PDF that contains two or more pages into InDesign, first make sure that you don't have any frames selected in InDesign. Then choose Place from the File menu and make sure your Show Import Options checkbox is checked. Choose a PDF with two or more pages; when you click Open you'll get the Place PDF dialog box. You can then choose to place all of the pages or select a page range. Once you click OK you can place each page into existing frames or you can have InDesign create the frames for you on the fly.

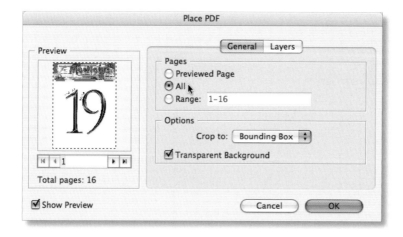

SAVE BACK TO INDESIGN CS

Not everyone moves to the new version of an application at once. You may be on InDesign CS2 and still have colleagues on InDesign CS. At first glance it may appear that there is no way to save an InDesign CS2 document back to CS. However, there is a way. What you need to do is choose Export from the File menu in InDesign CS2. When the Export dialog box appears, choose InDesign Interchange from the Format pop-up menu. Give the file a name, pick a location, and click Save. This creates an .inx file that InDesign CS can open (with the latest updates). Another use of the .inx format is for troubleshooting a problematic document. If you're having problems with an InDesign CS2 document, try exporting it to InDesign Interchange format. Then open it back up again in InDesign CS2 and save it with a different name. In effect, this will rebuild the document and that may solve your problem.

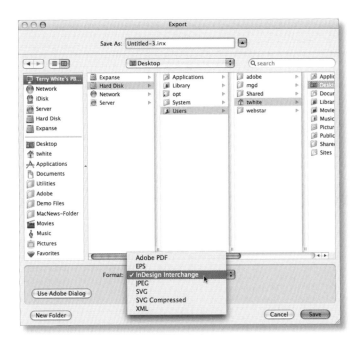

   MOVE PAGES DIALOG BOX

You can move pages around in the Pages palette easily enough by simply dragging them around. As long as you have a document with only a few pages, this works fine. However, if you have more pages than will fit in one window of the Pages palette, moving pages and having to scroll up and down can be a pain. The next time you find yourself in this situation, use the Move Pages dialog box instead. Bring up the Pages palette and choose Move Pages from the Pages palette menu. You can then specify a page range, and place them either before or after the page that you designate. This is way faster than drag-and-drop and it's much more efficient.

   LOCK COLUMN GUIDES

Locking and unlocking guides is probably second nature to you, and up until now it's been all or nothing. But let's say that you want to lock your column guides in place but still have the flexibility of moving your ruler guides around. The next time you find yourself in this situation, go to the Grids and Guides menu (under the View menu) and choose Lock Column Guides. This will lock only the column guides and leave you free to move your regular ruler guides around.

DATA MERGE

Data Merge is not technically new to InDesign; however, it is now included in InDesign CS2. Remember Mail Merge in your word processor? Mail Merge allows you to use a tab or comma delimited list and put fields in your form letter that automatically populate from the data in your list. Data Merge in InDesign CS2 takes this to a whole new level, allowing you to merge not only text, but images as well. First, define the list with the text that you want to populate your InDesign document. Then, in that list you need to include the path to each image on your hard drive for each record. Using the Data Merge palette (which is found under the Window menu, under Automation), you can drag the fields into your InDesign layout.

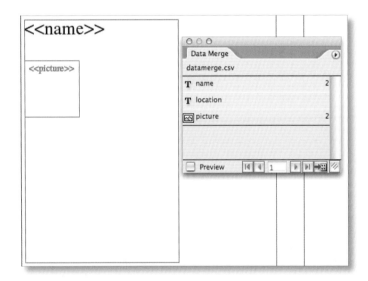

  CREATE PRINTER SPREADS

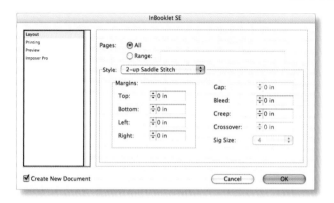

Another subtle change in InDesign CS2 is the inclusion of the InBooklet SE plug-in. Along with Data Merge, this plug-in was originally only available with the InDesign CS PageMaker Plug-in Pack. Now it's included in InDesign CS2. When you design your documents, you're likely in Reader Spreads (pages 1, 2, 3, 4, etc.). However, when you print your document for assembly in a book, it often needs to be in Printer Spreads (pages 8 & 1, 7 & 2, 6 & 3, etc.). Once your publication is designed, you can choose InBooklet SE from the File menu and set up your book. To verify your settings before actually generating the new document, click the Preview option on the left. Once you're satisfied, click OK and InDesign will build a new document for you.

  MULTI-PAGE EXPORT TO JPEG

Sometimes you just need a JPEG. With the Export JPEG feature in InDesign, you can now—with one command—export all your pages as individual JPEG files. Choose Export from the File menu and choose JPEG as the format from the pop-up menu at the bottom. Make sure you give it a file name and location and click the Save button. The next dialog box to appear will allow you to choose a page range and quality settings. When you click the Export button, InDesign CS2 will export each page as a separate JPEG in the location you chose.

Index

resizing, 28
rotating in frames, 240
rotating in tables, 201
scaling, 33–34
selecting, 46, 53
spacing. *See* spacing
special characters, 44
spell checking, 46–47
tracking, 32
transparent, 84
viewing overset, 240
word counts, 29
wrapping, 53, 126–127
text blocks
duplicating, 86
editing, 157
formatting, 35
text frames. *See also* **frames**
changing to graphics
frames, 111
fitting text in, 52
master page, 56
rotating, 240
speeding up, 54
thumbnails, 140
TIFF files, 170, 224
Toolbox, 12, 16
tools, 20. *See also specific tools*
tracking words, 32
transparency
identifying pages with, 144
layers and, 144
PDF files, 196
stacking order and, 144
text, 84

transparency flattener
preview, 148
transparency flattener styles,
145, 149
transparent items, printing, 148
type, 25–57. *See also* **fonts; text**
applying gradients to, 54
attributes, 30
defaults, 27
justification, 49
on paths, 26
preferences, 31
Type tool, 25, 55

U

Undo command, 175
unit of measurement, 141, 156,
164, 177
Units & Increments Preferences
dialog, 177
URLs, 190

V

vector graphics, 128
View All Spreads option, 20
vignettes, 122

W

warning dialogs, 22
Web, publishing on, 118, 228
Web authoring, 228
Websites, 189–190
word count feature, 29

Word files, 190, 239, 246
Word tables, 204
words. *See also* **text**
checking spelling of, 46–47
hyphenating, 48
keywords, 137–139
library searches, 138–139
selecting, 46
space between, 32
tracking, 32
workspace, custom, 16
wrapping text, 53, 126–127

Z

zero point, 166
Zoom field shortcut, 10
Zoom tool, 11
zooming
with Hand tool, 10
in/out, 153
specifying percentage amount
for, 9, 10
speed zooming, 8
undoing zooms, 2

creative **solutions**

It all starts here...

at **bhphotovideo.com** you'll find the latest products, award winning live support and worldwide shipping all at your finger tips. Or you can drop by our DreamStore at **420 9th Ave, New York City**

B&H
PHOTO · VIDEO · PRO AUDIO
800-336-7097

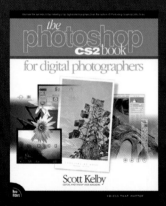
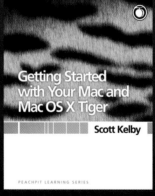